Drawn and Quartered

BY E. M. CIORAN

Anathemas and Admirations
Drawn and Quartered
History and Utopia
On the Heights of Despair
A Short History of Decay
Tears and Saints
The Temptation to Exist
The Trouble with Being Born

Drawn and Quartered

E. M. Cioran

Translated from the French by
Richard Howard

Foreword by
Eugene Thacker

Arcade Publishing
New York

Arcade Publishing books may be purchased in bulk at special discounts
for sales promotion, corporate gifts, fund-raising, or educational purposes.
Special editions can also be created to specifications. For details, contact the
Special Sales Department, Arcade Publishing, 307 West 36th Street,
11th Floor, New York, NY 10018 or arcade@skyhorsepublishing.com.

Originally published by Editions Gallimard, Paris, France, under the title
Ecartèlement

Arcade Publishing® is a registered trademark of Skyhorse Publishing, Inc.®,
a Delaware corporation.

Visit our website at www.arcadepub.com.

10 9 8 7 6 5 4 3

Library of Congress Cataloging-in-Publication Data is available on file.

ISBN: 978-1-61145-696-7
Ebook ISBN: 978-1-62872-493-6

Printed in China

Contents

Foreword

by Eugene Thacker

An informal meeting of friends outside a café – Paris,
winter, 1977. They are old schoolmates, each a Romanian
exile in France. Eugène Ionesco is a playwright and leading
figure of the so-called theater of the absurd; Mircea Eliade,
an historian of religion, is the author of *The Sacred and
the Profane*; and E. M. Cioran, wayward philosopher, is a
writer of aphorisms known for their dark wit and pessimistic
tone. Though their books are found on different shelves
in Parisian bookshops, they all speak to the key issues of
postwar Western culture – an existential crisis brought on by
a loss of faith in the humanist project; alienation from one's
self and others triggered by the chaotic pace of modern life;
weariness over the ascendency of scientific hegemony and
technical rationality; and an emerging awareness of a new
and unrecognizable world, a world at once post-industrial
and postmodern.

Cioran himself seemed especially aware of the
changing tides; the reclusive prowler of the Latin Quarter

began giving more and more interviews, some of them for radio and television. In 1979 Cioran published a book with the stark title *Écartèlement*, translated here as *Drawn and Quartered*. Cioran was in his late sixties, and had for decades been living modestly in his Rue de l'Odéon alcove with his companion, Simone Boué. *Drawn and Quartered* is, at first glance, classic Cioran – the sullen, pessimistic tone delivered in compact prose, writing situated in the interzone between philosophy and poetry. But this book is also exemplary of the later Cioran. The pessimistic statements are there, true, but there is a sharpness to them, a contentiousness absent in the earlier, more lyrical books: "Left to its own devices, depression would demolish even the fingernails"; "Nothing makes us modest, not even the sight of a corpse"; "Existing is plagiarism." The structure of the book is also a bit different. The first part of the book appears to be a series of polemical essays, while the second part comprises a string of taut, apocalyptic aphorisms. The two parts of the book are at once opposed to each other and yet form two sides of the same coin.

But, looking closely, we see that the essays are not just essays but border on agonistic, philosophical rants (the section entitled "The Urgency of the Worst" is exemplary in this regard – philosophy as a form of grumpiness). And the aphorisms are different too, far from the polished aphorisms of classical authors like La Rochefoucauld. They are more properly termed *fragments*, haphazard and incidental thoughts, more in the tradition of Pascal, Lichtenberg, and Kafka. Cioran's fragments are themselves so fragmented, so shattered (and shattering), that they sometimes seem less than a fragment: more a particle, a speck of dust, the debris of contemplation.

While Cioran was never one simply to react to trends, *Drawn and Quartered* shows a marked awareness with the late twentieth century concern with "the end" – the end of the millennium, the end of modernity, the end of history, the end of philosophy, the end of politics, the end of nature, the end of the "grand narratives" that we have traditionally told ourselves about a world ultimately indifferent to our made-up stories about it. "The obsession with *lastness* apropos of everything, *the last* as a category, as constitutive form of the mind, as original deformity, even as revelation. . . ." This awareness largely accounts for the eschatological tone of *Drawn and Quartered*: "It may be at hand, the day when, no longer able to endure the mass of fear we have accumulated, we shall collapse beneath the burden with which it overwhelms us." In passages like this, Cioran uncannily looks ahead to the postmodern melancholy of such thinkers as Jean Baudrillard, Paul Virilio, and even J. G. Ballard. "This time the fire from heaven will be *our* fire, and to escape it we shall rush to the depths of the earth, far from a world we ourselves have spoiled and disfigured." For Cioran, we can already hear the planetary death knell of a world selfishly made in our image, a human world for human beings.

But Cioran always adds a touch of black humor, a slight upward curl of the lips: "And we shall sojourn *beneath* the dead and envy their repose and their beatitude, those carefree skulls forever on vacation. . . ." If there is an epiphany in this book, it is not uplifting but a more difficult one that asks, not without humor, that we confront the strange human urge toward our own horizon, a horizon that ambivalently points to a non-human planet: "Enough to be in a crowd, in order to feel that you side with all the dead planets."

I

The Two Truths

According to a Gnostic legend, a war broke out in heaven among the angels, in which Michael's legions defeated those of the Dragon. The nonpartisan angels who had been content to look on were consigned to earth, in order to make there a choice they had not been able to determine on high, one all the more arduous in that they brought with them no memory of the combat or, indeed, of their equivocal attitude.

Thus history's commencement can be traced to a qualm, and man resulted from an original . . . vacillation, from that incapacity, before his banishment, to take sides. Cast to earth in order to learn how to choose, he was condemned to action, to risk, and was apt for it only insofar as he stifled the spectator in himself. Heaven alone permits neutrality to a certain point, while history, quite the contrary, appears to be the punishment of those who, before their incarnation, had found no reason to join one camp rather than another. We realize why human beings are so eager to espouse causes, to club together, to rally round a truth. Around what kind of truth?

In later Buddhism, especially in the Madyamika school, emphasis is placed on the radical opposition between real truth or *paramartha*, attribute of the delivered, and ordinary truth or *samvriti*, "veiled" truth or more exactly "truth of error," privilege or curse of the nonliberated.

Real truth, which assumes every risk, including that of the negation of all truth and of the idea of truth itself, is the prerogative of the inactive, who deliberately put themselves outside the sphere of action and for whom only the apprehension (whether instantaneous or methodical is of no importance) of insubstantiality matters, an apprehension accompanied by no feeling of frustration, rather the contrary, for access to nonreality implies a mysterious enrichment. For them history will be a bad dream to which they resign themselves, for nightmares are not a matter of choice. In order to grasp the essence of the historical process, or rather its *lack* of essence, we must acknowledge that all posthistorical truths are truths of error because they attribute a proper nature to what possesses nothing of the kind, a substance to what cannot have one. The theory of a double truth permits us to discern the place history occupies in the scale of unrealities, paradise of sleepwalkers, galloping obnubila-

4

sumption of gods, and of the surrogates for gods. Ancient China and Egypt wallowed for millennia in a magnificent sclerosis. As did African societies, before contact with the West. They too are threatened, because they have adopted another rhythm. Having lost the monopoly on stagnation, they grow increasingly frantic and will inevitably topple like their models, like those feverish civilizations incapable of lasting more than a dozen centuries. In the future, the peoples who accede to hegemony will enjoy it even less: history in slow motion has inexorably been replaced by history out of breath. Who can help regretting the pharaohs and their Chinese *colleagues?*

Institutions, societies, civilizations differ in duration and significance, yet all are subject to one and the same law, which decrees that the invincible impulse, the factor of their rise, must sag and settle after a certain time, this decadence corresponding to a slackening of that energizer which is . . . delirium. Compared with periods of expansion, of dementia really, those of decline seem sane and are so, are too much so—which makes them almost as deadly as the others.

A nation that has fulfilled itself, that has expended its talents and exploited the last resources of its genius, expiates such success by producing nothing *thereafter.* It has done its duty, it aspires to vegetate, but to its cost it will not have the latitude to do so. When the Romans—or what remained of them—sought repose, the Barbarians got under way, *en masse*. We read in a history of the invasions that the German tribes serving in the Empire's army and administration assumed Latin names until the middle of the fifth century. After which, Germanic names became a requirement. Exhausted, in retreat on every front, the masters were no longer feared, no longer respected. What was the use of bearing their names? "A fatal somnolence reigned everywhere," observed Salvian, bitterest censor of the ancient deliquescence in its final stages.

~

In the Métro, one evening, I looked closely around me: everyone had come from somewhere else . . . Among us, though, two or three faces *from here*, embarrassed silhouettes that seemed to be apologizing for their presence. The same spectacle in London.

Today's migrations are no longer made by compact displacements but by successive infiltrations: little by little, individuals insinuate themselves among the "natives," too anemic and too distinguished to stoop to the notion of a "territory." After a thousand years of vigilance, we open the gates . . . When one thinks of the long rivalries between the French and the English, then between the French and the Germans, it seems as if each nation, by weakening one another, had as its task to speed the hour of the common downfall so that other specimens of humanity may relay them. Like its predecessor, the new *Völkerwander-ung* will provoke an ethnic confusion whose phases cannot be distinctly foreseen. Confronted with these disparate profiles, the notion of a community homo-geneous to whatever degree is inconceivable. The very possibility of so heteroclite a crowd suggests that in the space it occupies there no longer existed, among the *indigenous,* any desire to safeguard even the shadow of an identity. At Rome, in the third century of our era, out of a million inhabitants, only sixty thousand were of Latin stock. Once a people has ful-filled the historical idea which was its mission to in-carnate, it no longer has any excuse to preserve its difference, to cherish its singularity, to safeguard its features amid a chaos of faces.

Having governed two hemispheres, the West is now becoming their laughingstock: subtle specters, end of the line in the literal sense, doomed to the sta-tus of pariahs, of flabby and faltering slaves, a status which perhaps the Russians will escape, those *last* White Men. Because they still have some pride, that motor, no, that *cause* of history. When a nation runs out of pride, when it ceases to regard itself as the rea-son or excuse for the universe, it excludes itself from becoming. It has *understood*—for its well-being or woe, depending on each one's perspective. If it now con-stitutes the despair of the ambitious, on the other hand it fascinates the meditative who happen to be a touch depraved. Dangerously advanced nations are the only ones that deserve interest, especially when we sustain ambiguous relations with Time and court Clio out of a need to punish ourselves. Moreover it is this need that incites us to undertake . . . anything, great or insignificant. Each of us labors *against* his interests: we are not conscious of this so long as we work, but examine any period and we see that action and sacrifice are almost always undertaken for a virtual or a declared enemy: the men of the Revolution for Bonaparte, Bonaparte for the Bourbons, the Bourbons for the Orleanists . . . Can history inspire only sneers—has it no goal? Yes, more than one, many in fact, but it achieves them *in reverse.* The phenomenon is universally verifiable. We realize the opposite of what we have pursued, we advance counter to the splendid lie we have made to ourselves; whence the interest of biographies, least boring of the suspect genres. The *will* has never served anyone: the most arguable of our productions is what we cling to most tenaciously, the motive for inflicting our worst privations on ourselves. This is true of a writer as well as of a conqueror, of any man in the street. The end of "anyone" suggests as many reflexions as the end of an empire, or of man himself, so proud of having acceded to the vertical position and so apprehensive of losing it, of returning to his earliest aspect, of concluding his career, in short, as he had begun it: stooping and shaggy. Over each being hangs the threat of regressing to his point of departure (as though to illustrate the uselessness of his trajectory, of any trajectory), and he who succeeds in evading it gives the impression of scamping a duty, of refusing to play the game by inventing an overly paradoxical mode of failure.

≠

The role of periods of decline is to lay a civilization bare, to unmask it, to strip it of the glamour and arrogance linked to its achievements. Thereby it can discern what it was worth and is worth now, what was illusory in its efforts and its convulsions. Insofar as it detaches itself from the fictions that guaranteed its fame, it will take a considerable stride toward knowledge . . . , toward disillusion, toward a generalized awakening, that fatal promotion which will project it outside of history (unless it is "awakened" simply by having ceased to be present there, to excel there). The universalization of awakening, fruit of lucidity, itself fruit of the erosion of reflexes, is the sign of emancipation in the order of the mind and of capitulation in the order of action, of history, in fact, itself no more than an acknowledgment of collapse: as soon as we turn our eyes upon history, we are in the situation of a dismayed spectator. The mechanical correlation established between *history* and *meaning* is the perfect example of the truth of error. History involves a meaning, if you like, but this meaning constantly belies and refutes it and thereby makes history piquant and sinister, pitiable and grandiose, in short, irresistibly demoralizing. Who would take history seriously if it were not the very road to degradation? The mere fact of being concerned with it tells everything about what it is, one's consciousness of history being, according to Erwin Reisner, a symptom of the end of time *(Geschichtsbewusstsein ist Symptom der Endzeit)*. We cannot, as it turns out, be obsessed with history without falling into an obsession with its conclusion. The theologian reflects on events *with a view* to the Last Judgment; the anxious man (or the prophet), with a view to a less sumptuous but quite as important decor. Both anticipate a calamity analogous to the one which the Delaware Indians projected into the past, and during which, according to their traditions, not only men prayed in terror, but the beasts as well. And the periods of calm? it will be objected. Undeniably they exist, though serenity is but a brilliant nightmare, no more than a Calvary that has *come off*.

Impossible to concede that the tragic is the individual's lot, and not that of history. Far from escaping it, history is subject to the tragic and marked by it even more than the tragic hero himself, the way it will *come out* being at the center of the curiosity it provokes. We are fascinated by history because we know by instinct what surprises lie in wait for it, and what splendid issue it offers to apprehension . . . For an informed mind, however, it adds little to the insoluble, to the original no-exit. Like tragedy, history resolves nothing, because there is nothing to resolve. It is always by failure that we study the future. Too bad we cannot breathe as if events, in their totality, were suspended! Each time they evidence themselves a little too much, we suffer a fit of determinism, of fatalistic rage. By free will we explain only the *surface* of history, the appearances it assumes, its external vicissitudes, but not its depths, its real course, which preserves, in spite of everything, a baffling, even a mysterious character. We are still amazed that Hannibal, after Cannae, did not fall upon Rome. Had he done so, we should be boasting today of our Carthaginian ancestry. To maintain that whim, that accident, hence the individual, play no part, is folly. Yet each time we envisage the future as a totality, the verdict of the *Mahabharata* invariably comes to mind: "The knot of Destiny cannot be untied; nothing in this world is the result of our actions."

ﺴ

Victims of a double sorcery, torn between the two truths, doomed to be unable to choose one without immediately regretting the other, we are too clear-sighted not to be deflated, disabused of illusion and of the lack of illusion, hence close to Rance,[2] who, a prisoner of his past, devoted his hermit's existence to arguing with those he had left behind, with the authors of lampoons who had questioned the sincerity of his conversion and the justice of his enterprises, thereby showing that it was easier to reform the Trappist Order than to abstain from the world. Similarly, nothing easier than to denounce history; on the other hand, nothing more arduous than to win free of it, for it is from history that we emerge and it will not let us forget it. History is the obstacle to ultimate revelation, the shackle we can strike off only if we have perceived the nullity of every event except the one that this very perception represents, and thanks to which we attain at moments to "the real truth," *i.e.*, to the victory over all truths. It is then that we understand Mommsen's [3] words: "A historian must be like God, he must love everyone and everything, even the devil." In other words, cease to prefer, occupy yourself with absence, with the obligation to be nothing ever again. We may imagine *the delivered* as a historian suddenly stricken with intemporality.

Our only choice is between irrespirable truths and salutary frauds. The truths that allow of no existence alone deserve the name of truths. Superior to the exigencies of the living, they do not condescend to be our accomplices. They are "inhuman" truths, truths of

14

vertigo, and we reject them because no one can do without props disguised as slogans or as gods. What is painful is to see that in each period it is the iconoclasts or those who claim to be such who most often resort to fictions and to lies. The ancient world must have been terribly afflicted to need so crude an antidote as the one Christianity was to administer. The modern world is just as badly off, judging by the remedies from which it expects miracles. Epicurus, the least fanatic of the wise, was the great loser then, as he is today. One is filled with amazement and even with dread when one hears men speak of freeing Man. How might slaves free the Slave? And how to believe that history—a procession of delusions—can drag on much longer? Soon it will be closing time in the gardens everywhere.

The Addict of Memoirs

The mystics, making a distinction between inner and outer man, necessarily opted for the former, *real being par excellence*; the latter, dismal or ludicrous puppet, fell by rights to the moralists, his accusers yet his accomplices, repelled and attracted by his nullity, incapable of transcending the equivocal save by bitterness, that second-rate melancholy which only a Pascal resists because he is always superior to his disgusts. And it is because he is always superior that Pascal would not affect the authors of memoirs, whereas the contagious acrimony of a La Rochefoucauld colors all their portraits and all their narratives.

Since he never raises his voice nor forces the tone, the moralist is naturally well brought up and he proves it by execrating his kind with elegance and, a more important detail, by writing little . . . Is there a better sign of "civilization" than laconism? To stress, to explain, to prove—so many forms of vulgarity. Anyone who pretends to a minimum of *tenue*, far from fearing sterility·must apply himself to it, must scuttle words in the name of the Word, must compound with silence, departing from it only by moments and the better to fall back into it. The *maxim*, however dubious it may be as a genre, nonetheless constitutes an exercise in modesty, since it permits us to wrest ourselves from the drawbacks of verbal plethora. Less demanding, because less condensed, the *portrait* is generally a sort of maxim, diluted in some cases, padded in others; yet it can, under exceptional circumstances, assume the rhythm of an *exploded* maxim, evoking infinity by the accumulation of features and the will to be exhaustive: we are then in the presence of a phenomenon without analogy, of a *case*, that of a writer who, by dint of feeling too confined in a language, transcends it and escapes from it—with all the words it contains . . . He does them violence, uproots them, takes them into himself, in order to do with them what seems best to himself without consideration for them or for the reader, upon whom he inflicts an unforgettable, a magnificent martyrdom. How ill-bred Saint-Simon is! . . . But no more than Life, to which he is, if one may say so, the literary counterpart. No weakness for abstraction, no *classical* stigma in him; comfortable with immediacy, his very senses are witty, and if he is often unfair, he is never false. All other portraits, next to his, seem schemas, stylized compositions that lack energy and veracity. His great trump: he never suspected he had genius, he did not know that limit-case of servitude. Nothing embarrasses him, nothing intimidates him; he forges ahead, letting himself be carried away by his frenzy, without inventing scruples or hesitations. An equatorial sensibility, ravaged by his outbursts, helpless to impose on himself those shackles that follow upon deliberation or withdrawal into oneself. No design, no precise contour. When you suppose you are reading an encomium, you are abruptly disabused; suddenly an unforeseen feature appears, an adjective that belongs to pamphleteering; in fact, it is neither an apology nor an execution you are reading, but the individual *as he is,* elementary and tortuous, spewed up by Chaos in the midst of Versailles.

Mme du Deffand,[4] who had read the *Memoirs* in manuscript, found their style "abominable." Such was doubtless the opinion of Duclos [5] as well, who had also frequented them in order to pilfer their details about the Regency, whose history he wrote in a language of exemplary insipidity: a kind of edulcorated Saint-Simon, his is the grace that extinguishes vigor. By its arid clarity, by its rejection of the unexpected and the incorrect, of the abstruse and the arbitrary, eighteenth-century style suggests a collapse *into perfection,* into nonlife. A hothouse product, artificial and bloodless, which, repugnant to any excess, could in no way produce a work of a total originality, with all that this implies of the impure or the dismaying.

On the other hand, a great quantity of works displaying a diaphanous discourse, without extensions or enigmas, a verbality turned anemic, superintended, censured by fashion, by the Inquisition of limpidity.

⌐

"I have insufficient leisure to have taste as well." This phrase—attributed to some personage, I no longer remember who—exceeds the range of mere wit. Taste, in fact, is the appanage of the idle, of dilettantes, of those who, having time on their hands, employ it upon subtle trifles and studied futilities, of those especially who use it against themselves.

"One morning (it was a Sunday) we were waiting for the Prince de Conti, in order to go to Mass; we were in the salon, sitting round a table on which we had all set our books of hours, which Mme la Maréchale (the Maréchale of Luxembourg) was leafing through. Suddenly she paused over two or three particular prayers which seemed to her in *the worst possible taste*, and whose expressions, indeed, were bizarre to say the least." (Mme de Genlis:[6] *Memoirs*)

What could be more ludicrous than to require a prayer to sacrifice to language, to be *written?* Instead it should be clumsy, a little stupid, in other words *true*. This quality was not particularly prized by minds sharpened on pirouettes, and which went to Mass in the same mood as to dinner or the hunt. Gravity, indispensable to piety, they lacked altogether; they liked and cultivated only the *exquisite*. The Maréchale's remark relates her to that Renaissance cardinal who claimed he was too fond of Virgil's Latin to be able to endure that of the Gospels, so clumsy . . . Certain delicacies are incompatible with faith: taste and the absolute are mutually exclusive . . . No god survives the mind's smile, the frivolity of a certain doubt; on the other hand, flagellating doubt wants only to deny itself, to become fervor. No use seeking this kind of metamorphosis in a world where refinement participates in a certain acrobatics.

By the mechanism of its genesis, by its very nature, each language contains certain metaphysical possibilities; French, especially that of the eighteenth century, includes almost none: its provocative, inhuman clarity, its refusal of the indeterminate, of any essential, tormenting obscurity, make it a means of expression which can strain after mystery but never truly accede to it. Moreover in French, mystery, like vertigo, if it is not postulated, if it is not willed, most often results from a defect of mind or a syntax adrift.

A dead language, one linguist observes, is a language in which we have no right to make mistakes. Which means we have no right to effect the slightest innovation. In the Enlightenment, French had reached this extreme limit of rigidity and fulfillment. After the Revolution, it became less rigorous and less pure; but it gained in naturalness what it lost in perfection. In

Drawn and Quartered

order to survive, to perpetuate itself, French needed to become corrupt, enriched by many a new impropriety, to move from the salon into the street. Thereby, its sphere of influence diminished. It could be the language of cultivated Europe only at a period when, singularly impoverished, it had reached its apogee of transparency. A discourse approaches universality when it frees itself from its origins, leaves them behind, disavows them: having reached this point, if it would reinvigorate itself, avoid unreality or sclerosis, it must renounce its own exigencies, break its forms and its models, it must condescend to *bad taste*.

Throughout the eighteenth century unfolds the spellbinding spectacle of a decrepit society, prefiguration of humanity at its term, permanently cured of all tomorrows. The absence of future, ceasing then to be the monopoly of one class, would extend to all, in a superb democratization by vacuity. No need to make an effort of imagination in order to represent this ultimate stage: more than one phenomenon affords such a notion. The very concept of progress has become inseparable from that of *dénouement*. The peoples of the world seek initiation into the art of self-destruction, and are impelled by such avidity that, in order to satisfy it, they will reject any formula likely to limit it. At the century's end rose the scaffold; at the

22

end of history, we can imagine a decor on another scale.

Every society flattered by the prospect of its end will succumb to the first blows; stripped of any principle of life, left nothing which might permit it to resist the assailing powers, it will yield to the charm of *débâcle*. If the Revolution triumphed, it did so because power was a fiction and the "tyrant" a phantom: it literally did battle against specters. Further, *any* revolution prevails only if it pits itself against an *unreal* order. The same is true of any advent, any great historical turning point. The Goths did not conquer Rome, they conquered a corpse. The Barbarians' only merit was to have had a nose . . .

The Regent, Philippe d'Orléans, at the beginning of the eighteenth century, was a perfect symbol of its high corruption. What first strikes us about him is his complete lack of "character." He dealt with affairs of State with the same casualness as private affairs: either kind interested him only as a consequence of the witticisms they occasioned. As inconsistent in his passions as in his vices, he yielded to them out of unconcern, and as though out of incuriosity. Incapable of loving or of hating either, he lived without invoking talents which were considerable but which he disdained to cultivate. "Lacking continuity in anything, to the point of being unable to realize one might possess such a thing," he was, Saint-Simon adds, of an "insensitivity which rendered him without malice in the most mortal and dangerous offenses; and since the nerve, the principle of hatred and friendship, of gratitude and vengeance, is one and the same, and since he was altogether deficient in this principle, the consequences were infinite and pernicious."

Deliquescent and ineffectual, of a miraculous listlessness, the Regent carried frivolity to the point of paroxysm, inaugurating thereby an era of hypercivilized freaks, bewitched by catastrophe and worthy to perish in it. A great disorder in affairs of State was to result. His contemporaries did not hesitate to make him responsible for it, they even dared compare him with Nero; yet they should have shown him more indulgence and considered themselves fortunate to undergo an absolutism attenuated by apathy and farce. That he was the tool of thieves, the Abbé Dubois[7] chief among them, is undeniable; but is not the negligence of smiling toads worth more than the vigilance of incorruptibles? Assuredly he lacked nerve; on the other hand, this inadequacy is a virtue, since it makes possible freedom or at least its simulacrum.

The Abbé Galiani (of whom Nietzsche was to make such a great case) is one of the rare men to have understood that in a moment when some thundered against oppression, the gentleness of manners was nonetheless a reality. To Louis XIV, obtuse and intractable, he had no hesitation to prefer Louis XV, fluctuating and skeptical. "When we compare the cruelty of the Jesuits' persecution of Port-Royal to the mildness with which the Encyclopedists were attacked, we see the difference in the reigns, the manners, and the hearts of the two kings. The former was a seeker after renown and mistook outcry for glory; the latter was an honest man who worked at the vilest of trades, that of king, as reluctantly as he could. We shall nowhere meet with such reign for many a day."

But what the Abbé seems not to understand is that if tolerance is desirable and if in and of itself it justifies the trouble one takes to live, on the other hand it turns out to be a symptom of weakness and dissolution. This tragic evidence could not compel recognition from a man who frequented those illusion-mongers, the Encyclopedists; it was to become striking in a more disabused, a more recent age . . . Society at that time, as we now know, was tolerant because it lacked the vigor necessary to persecute, hence to preserve itself. Of Louis XIV, Michelet once said that "in his soul *nothingness* had its place." With even more reason he might have said the same thing of Louis XVI. Here is the explanation of a marvelous and doomed epoch; the secret of the gentleness of manners is a fatal secret.

The Revolution was provoked by the abuses of a class disabused of everything, even of its privileges, to which it clung by reflex, without passion or insistence, for it had an ostensible weakness for the ideas of those who were to annihilate it. Accommodation of the adversary is the distinctive sign of debility, *i.e.*, of tolerance, which is, in the last analysis, only a *coquetry of the dying.*

"You are a woman of some experience," wrote the Marquise du Deffand to the Duchesse de Choiseul[8], "but you lack one sort that I hope you may never know: the privation of feeling, and the pain of being unable to do without it."

The age, at the apogee of artifice, had a nostalgia for *naïveté,* for the one condition it lacked most. At the same time, whatever authentic sentiments it had were attached to the savage, the rustic, or the silly, models inaccessible to minds ill-equipped to wallow in "stupidity," even in simplicity. Once sovereign, intelligence turns against all values alien to its exercise and offers no semblance of reality to cling to. He who dedicates himself to it by belief or even mania infallibly reaches the point of "lack of feeling" and regret for having committed oneself to an idol that bestows only the void, as is testified by the letters of Mme du Deffand, a matchless document with regard to the scourge of lucidity, the exasperation of consciousness, the debauch of interrogations and perplexities besetting the man cut off from everything, the man who has ceased to be *natural.* As ill-luck would have it, once lucid we become ever more so: no way of cheating or even retreating. And this progress is effected to the detriment of vitality, of instinct. "Neither romance nor temperament," the Marquise said of herself. We understand why her liaison with the Regent did not last more than two weeks. They were just alike, dangerously external to their own sensations. Does not boredom, their common torment, flourish in the abyss that opens between the mind and the senses? No more spontaneous movements, no more unconsciousness. "Love" is the first to suffer. Chamfort's[9] definition of it is perfectly suited to a period of "fantasy" and "epidermis" in which a Rivarol[10] boasted of being able, at the climax of a certain convulsion, to solve a geometry problem. Everything was cerebral, even orgasm. A still graver phenomenon, this deterioration of the senses, instead of affecting only a few isolated creatures, became the deficiency, the scourge of an entire class, wasted by the constant use of irony.

Every impulse, as every manifestation, of release, involves a negative aspect: when we no longer bear any invisible . . . chain, when nothing is left to restrain us from within, when for lack of vigor, of innocence, we cannot forge new prohibitions, we shall constitute a mass of weaklings more expert in the exegesis than in the practice of sexuality. Not without danger do we accede to a high degree of consciousness, just as we do not strip ourselves with impunity of certain salutary constraints. However, if the excess of consciousness contributes to its increase, the excess of freedom, an equally deadly phenomenon in the opposite direction, invariably murders freedom. Hence an impulse of emancipation, in whatever realm, represents both a step forward and the beginning of a decline.

Just as a nation in which no one deigns to be a *domestic* is lost, so we can conceive of a humanity in which the individual, imbued with his uniqueness, will no longer accept a subaltern labor, however "honorable." (In his *Notebooks*, Montesquieu already remarked: "We can no longer endure any of the things that have a specific object: men of war cannot endure war; men of State, the State; and so with other things.") Despite everything, man continues and will continue until he has pulverized his last prejudice, and his last belief; when he finally brings himself to do so, dazzled and destroyed by his own audacity, he will find himself naked facing the abyss that follows upon the disappearance of all dogmas, and of all taboos.

He who would establish himself in reality or opt for a credo but fails to do so, will take revenge by mocking those who achieve such things spontaneously. Irony derives from a disappointed, unslaked appetite for *naïveté* which, by dint of failures, sharpens and grows venomous. It inevitably assumes a universal extension; and if it prefers to attack and thereby to undermine religion, it does so because it secretly suffers from the bitterness of being unable to believe. Even more pernicious is the acid, furious mockery that degenerates into a system and borders on self-destruction. When the Marquise de Prie[11] was exiled to Normandy in 1726, Mme du Deffand followed her there to keep her company; in his *History of the Regency*, Lemontey reports that "these two friends sent each other every morning the satiric verses each had composed against the other."

In a milieu where slander was *de rigueur* and

where people stayed up for fear of being alone ("There was nothing she would not do rather than to accept the affliction of going to bed," Duclos remarks of some woman of fashion), there could be nothing sacred but conversation, corrosive words, sallies apparently playful but with murderous intention. No one being spared, one could point, as a characteristic quality of the times, to the "decadence of admiration." Everything connects: without *naïveté*, without piety, no capacity to admire, to consider beings *in themselves*, in their original and unique reality, aside from their temporal accidents, admiration, that interior genuflection which implies neither humiliation nor a feeling of impotence, is the prerogative, the certitude and the salvation of the pure, of those, precisely, who do not haunt salons.

Only quarrelsome, indiscreet, jealous, refractory nations have an *interesting* history: that of France is so to a supreme degree. Fertile in events and, even more, in writers to discuss them, France is the providence of the addict of Memoirs.

The Frenchman is capricious or fanatical, he judges by whim or by system; yet even a system assumes in him the appearance of a whim. The characteristic that truly defines him is fickleness, cause of that parade of regimes of which he is an amused of frantic spectator, above all concerned to show that even in his rages he is never a dupe, alternately beneficiary and victim of that "literary spirit" that consists, according to Tocqueville, in seeking out "what is ingenious and new rather than what is true, in loving what produces a fine appearance rather than what serves, in showing oneself sensitive to the actors' proper performance and utterance regardless of the consequences of the play, and in reaching a conclusion, finally, on the basis of impressions rather than of reasons." (*Souvenirs*) And Tocqueville adds: "The French nation, taken as a whole, too often judges in politics as a man of letters."

The *littérateur* is less apt than anyone else to understand the functioning of the State; he shows a certain competence in doing so only during revolutions, precisely because authority is then abolished and, in the absence of power, he has the faculty of imagining that everything can be solved by attitudes or phrases. It is not so much free institutions that interest him as the counterfeits and quackery of freedom. Nothing surprising in the fact that the men of 1789 were inspired by an eccentric like Rousseau and not by Montesquieu, a solid mind with no love of divagation, a mind that cannot serve as a model for idyllic or bloodthirsty rhetoricians.

In Anglo-Saxon countries, religious sects permit the citizen to give free rein to his madness, to his need of controversy and scandal; whence religious diversity and political uniformity. In Catholic countries, on the contrary, the individual's *resources of unreason* can surface only in the anarchy of parties and of factions; it is here that he satisfies his appetite for heresy. No nation till now has found the secret for being *wise* in both politics and religion. Were this secret ever to be found, the French would be the last to seek to profit by it, they who, according to Talleyrand, made their Revolution *out of vanity*, a defect so deeply ingrained in their nature that it became a virtue, in any case an impulse that incites them to produce and to act, to *shine* above all; whence their *esprit*, an exhibition of the intelligence, a concern to outdo one's neighbor at any cost, to have the last word. But if vanity sharpens the faculties, making us avoid the commonplace and combat indolence, it unfortunately makes anyone subject to it into a man flayed alive; hence by the mortifications it inflicts upon them, the French have paid for all the advantages they have so abundantly enjoyed. For a thousand years, history has revolved around them: such a windfall is expiated; their punishment has been and remains the irritation of a self-love forever discontent, forever unappeased. When they were powerful, they complained of not being sufficiently so; now they complain of no longer being so at all. Such is the drama of a nation embittered in prosperity no less than in misfortune, insatiable and fickle, too favored by fate to know modesty or resignation, as unsuited to observe proportion in the face of the inevitable as of the unexpected.

After History

The end of history is inscribed in its beginnings—history, man at grips with time, bearing the stigmata that define both time and man.

Interrupted imbalance, ceaselessly dislocated being, time is in itself a drama of which history represents the most notable episode. For what is history, really, if not an imbalance, a swift, intense dislocation of time itself, a rush toward a future where nothing ever *becomes* again?

Just as theologians rightly speak of ours as a post-Christian age, some day we shall hear of the splendors and miseries of living in a posthistorical epoch. Despite everything, it would be sweet to know that twilight success in which we might escape the succession of generations and the parade of tomorrows, and when, on the ruins of historical time, existence, at last identical with itself, will again become what it was before turning into history. Historical time is so tense, so strained, that it is hard to see how it can keep from exploding. At each of its moments it gives the impression that it is on the point of breaking. Perhaps the accident will occur less precipitately than we hope. But it cannot fail to occur. And it is only then, after it has happened, that the beneficiaries, the epicures of posthistory will know what history was made of. "Henceforth there will be no more events!" they will exclaim. A chapter—the most curious of the entire cosmic unfolding—will thus be closed.

Obviously such a cry is conceivable only on terms of an imperfect disaster. Complete success would involve a radical simplification, in fact the suppression of the *future.* Rare are the catastrophes without a hitch: that should reassure the impatient, the feverish, the amateurs of great occasions, though in this case resignation is certainly *de rigueur.* Not to everyone was it granted to observe the Deluge *at close range.* One imagines the humor of those who, having anticipated it, did not live long enough to be able to witness it.

    ↜

In order to rein in the expansion of a flawed animal, the urgency of artificial scourges that will advantageously replace the natural ones is increasingly making itself felt, and to varying degrees seduces everyone. The End is gaining ground. We cannot go out into the street, look at the faces there, exchange words, hear the least rumble, without telling ourselves that the hour is near, even if it will sound only in a century or ten. A look of *dénouement* heightens the merest gesture, the most banal spectacle, the stupidest incident, and we should have to be refractory to the inevitable not to notice as much.

~

As long as history follows a more or less normal course, every event appears as a whim, a *faux pas* of Time; once it changes cadence, the slightest incident assumes the scope of a sign. Everything that happens then is equivalent to a symptom, a warning, the imminence of a conclusion. In the indifferent ages (in other words, in the absolute), the event—expression of a present that repeats, that multiplies itself—involves a significance *in itself* and seems not to unfold in time; on the contrary, in periods when the future is synonymous with deadly renewal, there is nothing that fails to evoke a progress toward the unheard-of, a vision related to that of the *Samyutta-Nikâya:* "The whole world is in flames, the whole world is wrapped in clouds of smoke, the whole world is devoured by fire, the whole world trembles." Mara, that sardonic monster, holds in her fangs and claws the wheel of birth and death, and in certain Tibetan figurations, her gaze perfectly translates the lust, the pursuit of evil, unconscious in nature, half-formulated in man, strikingly evident in gods—unappeasable pursuit whose manifestation, pernicious *par excellence*, remains for us that interminable parade of events with their inherent idolatries. Only the nightmare of history permits us to divine the nightmare of transmigration. With one reservation, however. For the Buddhist, the peregrination from existence to existence is a terror from which he seeks to detach himself; he labors to do so with all his might, sincerely terrified by the calamity of being reborn and dying again, which he would not for a moment dream of savoring in secret. No complicity, in him, with disaster, with the dangers which lie in wait for him without and especially within.

We, on the other hand, we compound with what threatens us, we cherish our anathemas, greedy for what pulverizes us; not for anything would we renounce our own nightmare to which we have assigned as many capital letters as we have known illusions. These illusions have been discredited, like the capital letters, but the nightmare remains, decapitated and naked, and we continue to love it precisely because it is ours and because we do not see what to replace it by. It is as if an aspirant to nirvana, weary of pursuing it in vain, were to turn away in order to wallow, to sink into *samsâra*, accomplice of his downfall, as we are of ours.

After History

Man makes history; in its turn history unmakes man. He is its author and its object, its agent and its victim. He has imagined hitherto that he masters it, now he knows that it escapes him, that it dissolves into the insoluble and the intolerable: a lunatic epic, whose conclusion implies no notion of finality. How to assign it a goal? If it had one, history would reach it only once it had reached its term. The only advantage will be enjoyed by the last of the race, the survivors, the *leftovers*, they alone are to be gratified, profiteers of the incalculable number of efforts and torments the past will have known. An overly grotesque and unjust vision. If we insist that history must have a meaning let us seek it in the curse that weighs upon it, and nowhere else. The isolated individual can have a meaning only to the degree that he participates in this curse. A maleficent genius presides over history's destinies. It plainly has no goal, but it is burdened by a fatality that replaces it, and which confers upon the future a simulacrum of necessity. It is this fatality, and this alone, that warrants our speaking without absurdity of a *logic of history*—and even of a providence, a special providence, it is true, suspect to a degree, whose designs are less impenetrable than those of the other one, reputed to be kindly. This suspect providence causes civilizations whose progress it governs always to depart from their original direction in order to attain the contrary of their goals, in order to decline with an obstinacy and a method which clearly betray the maneuvers of a dark and ironic power.

⌐

According to some, history is only in its early stages; they forget that it is an exceptional phenomenon, necessarily ephemeral, a luxury, an interlude, a deviation . . . By giving rise to it, by investing it with his substance, man has expended himself, reduced himself, weakened himself. So long as, having escaped his origins, he nevertheless remained close to them, he could *endure* without danger; once he turned from them and proceeded to flee them, he entered upon a necessarily brief career: a few wretched millennia . . . History, his work, having become independent of him, exhausts him, devours him, and will not fail to crush him altogether. And he will succumb with it, ultimate *débâcle*, just punishment for so many usurpations and follies, rising out of the temptation of Titanism. The enterprise of Prometheus is compromised forever. Man, having violated every unwritten law, the only ones that count, and crossed every frontier assigned to him, has mounted too high not to excite the jealousy of the gods who, determined to strike him down, wait for him now at the crossroads. The consummation of the historical process is henceforth inexorable, without our being able to say, for all that, if it will be lingering or lightninglike. Everything indicates that humanity is going downhill, despite its successes or rather because of them. If it is relatively easy to single out, for any distinct civilization, the moment of its apogee, the same is not true for the historical process as a whole. What was its summit? And where to situate it—the first centuries of Greece, India or China, or at a certain date in the West? Impossible to decide without advancing excessively personal preferences.

In any case it is manifest that man has given the best of himself, and that even if we were to witness the emergence of other civilizations, they would certainly not be worth the ancient ones, nor even the modern ones, not counting the fact that they could not avoid the contagion of the end, which has become for us a kind of obligation and program. From prehistory to ourselves, and from ourselves to posthistory, such is the road toward a gigantic fiasco, prepared and announced by every period, including apogee epochs. Even utopianists identify the future with a failure, since they invent a regime supposed to escape any kind of *becoming*: their vision is that of *another* time within time . . . , something like an inexhaustible failure, unbroached by temporality and superior to it. But history, of which Ahriman[12] is the master, tramples such divagations and is loath to envisage the possibility of a paradise, even a lost one—that strips all utopias of their object and their reason for being. How revealing that we come up against this notion of paradise as soon as we want to grasp history in its own nature. It is because we cannot apprehend its originality without referring to its antipodes, history appearing as a gradual negation, as a progressive removal from a first condition, from an initial miracle, altogether conventional and bewitching: *kitsch* founded on nostalgia. When this progress toward the end is completed, history will have achieved its "goal": it will no longer keep anything within itself that can recall its point of departure, concerning which it is of little importance that it be merely a fable. Paradise, conceivable at best in the past, is not so at all in the future: the fact nonetheless that it has been placed *before* history throws a devastating light on the latter, so that we may well ask if it wouldn't have been better for history to remain in the state of threat, of pure virtuality . . .

It is less urgent to probe "the future," merely an object of dread, than the *end*, what will come after "the future," when historical time, coextensive with the human enterprise, having ceased, the procession of nations and empires will also thereby cease. Relieved of the burden of history, man, at the pinnacle of exhaustion, once he has abdicated his singularity, will no longer possess anything but an empty consciousness without anything that might fill it: a disabused troglodyte, a troglodyte which has shed everything. Will he reconnect with his remote ancestors, will posthistory appear as an aggravated version of prehistory? And how to establish the physiognomy of this survivor, whom the cataclysm will have brought back to the caves? What could he do facing these two extremes, confronting that interval which separates them, in which was elaborated a heritage he rejects? Disengaged from all values, from all the fictions current during that lapse of time, he neither could nor would, in his lucid decrepitude, invent new ones. And thus the game that had hitherto ruled the succession of civilizations will be ended.

~

After so many feats and conquests, man is beginning to put himself out of date. He still deserves some interest only insofar as he is tracked and cornered, sinking ever deeper. If he continues, it is because he hasn't the strength to capitulate, to suspend his desertion *forward* (the very definition of history), because he has acquired an automatism within decline. We shall never know exactly what has broken in him, but there is a break, it is there. It was there from the beginning, one might allege. No doubt, but vestigial, and he, in his early strength, readily accustomed himself to it. It was not that yawning fracture, product of a long labor of self-destruction, the specialty of a subversive animal which, having for such a long time undermined everything, was to finish by undermining itself. Subversion of man's foundations (which is how any *analysis*, psychological or otherwise, concludes), of his "ego," of his state as a subject, his rebellions camouflaging the blows he aims at himself. What is sure is that he is stricken in his depths, that he is rotten to the roots. Moreover we do not feel ourselves to be

41

truly men except when we become aware of this essential rottenness, partly masked hitherto but increasingly perceptible since man has explored and exploded his own secrets. By dint of becoming transparent to himself, he can no longer undertake anything, "create" anything, and this will be a desiccation by insufficient blindness, by an extermination of *naïveté*. Where will he still find enough energy to persevere in a task that requires a minimum of freshness, of obnubilation? If he sometimes manages to delude himself on his own account, he no longer deludes himself at all about the human adventure. What foolishness to assert that he is only beginning! In reality he proceeds, an almost supernatural wreck, toward a limit condition: a sage *corroded* by wisdom . . . He is rotten, yes, gangrenous, and all of us with him. We advance *en masse* toward a confusion without analogy, we shall rise up one against the other like convulsive defectives, like hallucinated puppets, because, everything having become impossible and unbreathable for us all, no one will deign to live except to liquidate and to liquidate himself. The sole frenzy we are still capable of is the frenzy of the end. Then will come a supreme form of stagnation when, roles played, stage abandoned, we can ruminate the epilogue at leisure.

What disgusts us with history is to think that, according to a famous remark, what we see today will someday be history . . . We should never set store by what *happens,* and it indicates a certain derangement that we do so. Yet if we arm ourselves with scorn, how to *animate* anything at all? The true historian, a fidgety man who wears the mask of objectivity, suffers and strives to suffer, and this is why he is so present in his narratives or his formulas. Far from regarding from on high the horrors he had to describe, Tacitus wallowed in them, and, a fascinated accuser, magnified them wantonly. Unsated by anomaly, he grew bored as soon as injustice and crime diminished. He knew, as later Saint-Simon was to know, the delights of indignation, the pleasures of rage. Hume regarded him as the deepest mind of Antiquity—let us say the most vital, and the closest to us by the quality of his masochism, that vice or talent indispensable to anyone who considers human affairs, whether a newspaper filler or the Last Judgment.

Consider carefully the merest event: in the best of cases, the positive and negative elements that participate in it balance out; generally the negatives predominate. Which is to say, it would have been preferable that it not take place. We should then have been dispensed from taking part in it, enduring it. What is the good of *adding* anything at all to what is or seems to be? History, a futile odyssey, has no excuse, and on occasion we are tempted to inculpate art itself, however imperious the need from which it emanates. To produce is accessory; what matters is to draw on one's own depths, to be oneself in a total fashion, without stooping to any form of expression. To have built great cathedrals derives from the same error as to have waged great battles. Better to try to live *in depth* than to advance through centuries toward a *débâcle*.

Certainly, there is no salvation by history. Never our fundamental dimension, it is only the apotheosis of appearances. Supposing our external career could once and for all be abolished, would we rediscover our true nature? Will posthistoric man, an entirely vacant being, be likely to rejoin the intemporal in himself, *i.e.*, everything history has stifled in us? All that counts is our moments which it has not yet contaminated. The only beings in a position to understand each other, truly to communicate among themselves, are those who open themselves to such moments. The periods subject to metaphysical interrogation remain the culminating moments, the true summits of the past. The essential can be approached solely by internal exploits, which alone accede to it, if only for the interval of a second, which weighs more heavily than all the rest, than time itself.

"It was at Rome, on October 15, 1764, as I sat musing amid the ruins of the Capitol, while the barefoot friars were singing vespers in the Temple of Jupiter, that the idea of writing the history of the decline and fall of the city first started to my mind."

After History

Empires end either by disaggregation or by catastrophe or by some conjunction of the two. The same choice is offered to humanity in general. Let us imagine a future Gibbon, meditating on what humanity was, if it should turn out that there is still some historian at the end of not one cycle but of all. How would he go about describing our excesses, our demonic availabilities, the source of our dynamism—he who will be surrounded only by beings addicted to a holy inertia, at the term of a process of nameless deterioration, liberated forever from the madness of self-assertion, of leaving traces, of marking one's passage here on earth? Would he comprehend our incapacity to elaborate a static vision of the world and to abide by it, to emancipate ourselves from the idea and the obsession of action? What ruins us, no, what *has* ruined us, is the thirst for a destiny, for any destiny whatever: and this weakness, the key to any historical future, if it has destroyed us, if it has reduced us to nothingness, will at the same time have saved us by giving us a taste for collapse, a desire for an event to exceed all events, for a fear to surpass all fears. Catastrophe being the only solution, and posthistory, granting the hypothesis that it can come next, the sole issue and unique opportunity—it is legitimate to wonder if humanity as it is would not be better off eliminating itself now rather than fading and foundering in expectation, exposing itself to an era of agony in which it would risk losing all ambition, even the ambition to vanish . . .

Urgency of the Worst

Everything suggests the hypothesis that history will pass and, with it, the being to whose detriment it was constructed; that being once abided within itself—history dragged it out and associated it with its own convulsions; thus history represents the terrain where man has unceasingly declined, depreciated. That drama which was a reflection on history from the very beginning—how could it fail to affect it now that history approaches its term, and how could it fail to affect us, witnesses as we are to a last-act fever which, we must admit, is anything but disagreeable to us? In this we resemble the early Christians, so greedy for the worst. To their intense disappointment, the worst did not occur, for all the vaticinations that fill the writings of the period. The wilder the latter became, as though to urge God on, to force His hand, the more He, ravaged and undecided, hobbled Himself with His own scruples. In disarray, the faithful had to acknowledge the obvious: the new Advent would not occur, the Parousia was postponed; neither salvation nor damnation lay on the horizon. Under these conditions, what else could they do but wait, caught between resignation and hope, for better days, *the time of the end?* Better equipped than they, we have our end in hand, or at least within reach, and in order to precipitate its coming, we have no need of cooperation from on high. Yet bunglers as we are, we are unlikely to derive any advantage whatever from such a windfall. How have we come to be where we are? By what process, after so many reassuring centuries, do we find ourselves on the threshold of a reality which sarcasm alone renders tolerable? Since the Renaissance, humanity has merely evaded the ultimate meaning of its progress, the deadly principle manifest within it. The Enlightenment, in particular, was to furnish a fair contribution to this enterprise of obnubilation. Then in the next century came the idolatry of the Future, confirming the illusions of the one that preceded. To an age as disabused as ours, the Future persists in displaying its promises, though those who believe in them are rare indeed. Not that such idolatry is over and done with; but we are obliged to minimize, to disdain it—out of caution, out of fear. This is because we now know that the Future is compatible with the atrocious, that it even leads there or, at least, that it gives rise to prosperity and horror with equal facility. Since with each theory and each discovery we degrade ourselves a little further, what have we in common, still, with the "enlightened" breed, with the maniacs of the Possible? Newton's contemporaries were amazed that a mind of his order should lower itself to comment on the visions of the Apostle. Quite the reverse, for us it would be incomprehensible not to do so, and the man of science reluctant to engage in such an enterprise would call down our scorn upon his head. Further, he need not even lay much stress on the incriminated revelations; he lives them in his way, and prepares a new version of them, one more convincing and more effective than the original, for it is stripped of pomp and poetry. By dint of application, he distinguishes its contours so clearly that he feels a certain embarrassment about mentioning it. The end of time seeming to him a commonplace, what looks odd to him is not that such a thing should be conceivable but that it should be so long in occurring. He does his best to bring it about, to accelerate the catastrophe: is it his fault if it hesitates, if it tergiversates? No less impatient, we too long for it to come and deliver us from the curiosity which oppresses us so. Depending on our moods, we shift the date ahead or back, while, breathing in terms of the irrespirable, expanding in what stifles us, we already participate by all our thoughts, however luminous, in the Night in which they will capsize.

It may be at hand, the day when, no longer able to endure that mass of fear we have accumulated, we shall collapse beneath the burden with which it overwhelms us. This time the fire from heaven will be *our* fire, and to escape it we shall rush to the depths of the earth, far from a world we ourselves have spoiled and disfigured. And we shall sojourn *beneath* the dead and envy their repose and their beatitude, those carefree skulls forever on vacation, those calmed and modest skeletons, freed at last from the impertinences of the blood and the claims of the flesh. Swarming in the dark, we shall know at least the satisfaction of no longer having to look one another in the face, the bliss of losing our faces altogether. Exposed to the same tribulations and the same dangers, we shall all be alike, yet more alien to one another than we ever were.

To escape our fate—what is the good of striving for that? Not that we must despair of finding a substitute ending. Yet it must be a likely one, one that has some chance of being realized. Man being what he is, can we admit that he might be granted the opportunity of subsiding in the peace of decay, amid the benefits of decrepitude? Doubtless he already staggers under the burden of the millennia, yet it seems unlikely it will be his lot to bear this weight to the end, till the exhaustion of his strength. On the contrary, everything suggests that the luxury of dotage will be denied him, if only by reason of the rhythm by which he lives, his inclination to excess. Infatuated by his gifts, he flouts nature, breaks out of its stagnation, creating a chaos alternately vile and tragic that becomes strictly (and naturally) untenable. That he should clear out as soon as possible is surely nature's wish, and one that man, if he wanted to, could gratify on the spot. Hence nature would be rid of these seditious creatures whose every smile is subversive, of this antilife force she shelters by force, of this usurper who has stolen her secrets in order to subjugate and dishonor her. But man himself by his crimes and depredations was to fall into ignominy and bondage. Having exceeded, as much by his knowledge as by his actions, the limits assigned to the creature, he attacked the very sources of his being, his ultimate depths, his point of origin. His conquests are the doings of a traitor to life and to himself. Whence his guilty airs, his disturbed manners, whence the remorse he attempts to conceal by insolence and preoccupation. If he intoxicates himself by noise, it is to escape the charge which the slightest self-consciousness would press home. Creation rested in a sacred stupor, in an admirable and inaudible moan; shaking it up by his frenzy, his vociferations of a hunted monster, he has rendered it unrecognizable and forever compromised its peace. The disappearance of silence must be counted among the harbingers of the end. It is no longer on account of its shamelessness or its debauchery that today's Babylon the Great deserves to fall, but because of its racket and its noise, the stridency of its hardware and of the desperate types who cannot manage to quiet down. Rabid against the solitaries, those latest martyrs, she pursues them, tortures them, interrupts their ruminations at every moment, infiltrates herself into their thoughts like a noisy virus in order to undermine and disintegrate them. How, in their exasperation, could they not hope to see her collapse without delay?

This new whore contaminates space, corrupts beings and landscapes alike, drives out purity and meditation. Where to go? Where to live? And what to seek in the uproar of a Babylonized planet? Before it explodes, those who have suffered most here, those she has tormented, will finally have their revenge; they will be the only ones to bless the *dénouement*, the only ones to savor this suspension of the din, this brief and decisive silence preceding the great catastrophes.

The more power man acquires, the more vulnerable he becomes. What he must fear most is the moment when, creation entirely fleeced, he will celebrate his triumph, that fatal apotheosis, the victory he will not survive. Most likely he will disappear before having realized all his ambitions. He is so powerful already that we wonder why he aspires to be more so. So much insatiability betrays a wretchedness without recourse, a magisterial failure. Plants and creatures bear upon themselves the marks of salvation, as man those of perdition. This is true of each of us, of the Race as a whole, dazzled and crushed by the brilliance of the Incurable. Which is perpetuated through the nations, doomed to servitude by the simple automatism of becoming. All are ultimately only so many detours history makes in order to end with the establishment of a tyranny on a large scale, an empire that will include the continents. No more frontiers, no more *elsewheres* . . . hence no more freedom, no more illusions. It is significant that the Book of the End was

conceived at a moment when men, and the gods themselves, had to bow before Rome's caprice. The arbitrary having degenerated into terror, what else did the
oppressed have but the hope of being someday delivered from it by an event of cosmic dimensions, whose
main outlines, and even whose details, they busied
themselves imagining? In the empire to come, the disinherited will proceed in the same way; the visionary
genre, deliberately sinister, will for them supplant all
the others; but contrary to the early Christians, they
will not detest the new Nero—or rather they will detest
themselves in him, they will make him into an ab-
horred ideal, the first of the damned, none of them
having the nerve to posit themselves as the Chosen . . .

No new heaven, no new earth, and no new angel to open the "pit of the abyss." Moreover do we not
have the key to it ourselves? The abyss is in ourselves
and outside of ourselves, it is yesterday's presentiment, today's question, tomorrow's certainty. The
founding, like the dislocation, of the future empire
will take place amid disruptions without precedent in
the past. At the stage we have reached, even if we
should want to, it would be impossible to amend ourselves and, in a spasm of wisdom, to turn back . . . So
virulent is our perversity that instead of attenuating it,
our reflexions on it, like our efforts to surmount it,
confirm and aggravate it. Predestined to engulfment,
we represent, in the drama of creation, the most spec-
tacular and the most pitiable episode of all. Since in us

has awakened the evil that slumbered in the remainder of the living, it remains for us to destroy ourselves so that they might be saved. The virtualities of laceration and conflict that the others contained have become real and concentrated in us, and it is at our own expense that we have liberated plants and animals from the deadly elements that lay dormant within them. An act of generosity, a sacrifice to which we have consented only in order to regret it and upbraid ourselves. Jealous of their unconsciousness, basis of their salvation, we would be as they are, and furious at being unable to become so, we meditate their ruin, we strive to interest them in our misfortunes in order to revenge ourselves upon them. It is the animals we resent most of all: what would we not give to strip them of their silence, to convert them to language, to inflict upon them the abjection of speech! The charm of a life without reflexion, of existence *as such* being forbidden to us, we cannot bear that others should delight in it. Deserters of innocence, we turn against whoever still resides within it, against all the beings that, indifferent to our adventure, loll in their blessed torpor. And the gods—have we not turned against them as well, outraged to see that they were conscious without suffering from the fact, while for us consciousness and shipwreck are one and the same thing? If we have penetrated the secret of their power, we have not been able, on the other hand, to pierce that of their serenity. Vengeance was inevitable: how to forgive them for possessing knowledge without incurring the curse inherent in it? Now that they have disappeared, we have not thereby renounced the search for happiness: we have sought it and still search for it in precisely what distances it from us, in the conjunction of knowledge and arrogance. The closer these terms come to identity, the fainter become the vestiges we kept of our origins. Once we had fallen from the passivity in which we resided, in which we were at home, we engulfed ourselves in action, without the possibility of wrenching ourselves free of it or of regaining our true fatherland. If action has corrupted us, we have corrupted action in our turn: from this reciprocal degradation would result that defiance of contemplation which is history, a challenge coextensive with events and as lamentable as they. What was envisioned on Patmos we shall see with our own eyes one of these days, we shall distinctly perceive that sun "black as sackcloth of hair," and that moon of blood, those stars falling like figs, that sun "departing as a scroll when it is rolled together." Our anxiety echoes that of the Seer, whom we are closer to than were our forebears, including those who wrote on him, particularly the author of *The Origins of Christianity*[13], who was so rash as to assert "We know that the end of the world is not so near as the inspired prophets of the first century supposed, and that this end will not be a sudden catastrophe. It will occur by freezing, in thousands of centuries . . ." The semiliterate Evangelist saw more clearly than his learned commentator, adherent of modern superstitions. Nor should we be surprised at this: as we retrace our steps to remote antiquity, we encounter anxieties like our own. Philosophy, at its beginning, had more than the presentiment—it had the exact intuition of the completion, the expiration of the future. Heraclitus, our ideal contemporary, already knew that fire "will judge" everything; he even envisaged a general conflagration at the end of each cosmic period, a repeating cataclysm, a corollary to any cyclic conception of time. Less audacious and less exigent, we content ourselves with a *single* end, lacking the vigor that would allow us to conceive (and to endure) several such . . . We grant, it is true, a plurality of civilizations, so many worlds that are born and die; but who among us would consent to the indefinite recommencement of history in its totality? With each event that occurs, and which to us seems necessarily irreversible, we advance one step further toward a unique *dénouement,* according to the rhythm of the progress whose schema we adopt and whose twaddle, of course, we reject. We progress, yes, we even gallop toward a specific disaster, and not toward some mirific perfection. The greater our repugnance for the fables of our immediate predecessors, the closer we feel to the Orphics, who placed Night at the origin of things, or to an Empedocles, who conferred upon Hatred certain cosmogonic virtues. But it is in fact with the philosopher of Ephesus that we associate ourselves most closely, when he assures us that the universe is governed by the lightning. Reason no longer blinding us, we are finally discovering the other face of the world, the darkness that resides there, and if there must be a light that will turn us from it, such light will be, we no longer doubt it, that of some definitive fulguration. Another feature that brings us closer to the pre-Socratics is the passion for the ineluctable, which *they* conceived at the dawn of our civilization, at the first contact with the elements and beings whose spectacle must have plunged them into an amazed dread. At the term of the ages, we ourselves conceive of this passion as the only modality by which we may be reconciled with man, with the horror he inspires in us. Resigned or enchanted, we watch him running toward what denies him, trembling in the intoxication of his annihilation. Panic—his vice, his reason for being, the principle of his expansion, of his unhealthy prosperity—has so possessed him, has defined him so intimately, that he would perish on the spot were it to be withdrawn from him. Subtle as the first philosophers were, they could not divine that the moral universe would propose problems as insoluble and as terrifying as the physical universe: man, at the period when they "flourished," had not yet given his proofs . . . The advantage we have over them is to know of what he is capable, or, more specifically, of what we ourselves are capable. For that panic, at once so stimulating and so destructive, is what we all bear in ourselves, it is marked upon our countenances, explodes in our every gesture, traverses our bones and seethes in our blood. Our contortions, visible or secret, we communicate to the planet; already it trembles even as we do, it suffers the contagion of our crises and, as this *grand mal* spreads, it vomits us forth, cursing us the while.

It is doubtless distressing that we must confront the final phase of the historical process at the moment when, having liquidated our old beliefs, we lack any metaphysical assets, any substantial reserves of the Absolute. Surprised by the death agony, dispossessed of everything, we skirt that flattering nightmare experienced by all who had the privilege of finding themselves at the heart of a conspicuous *débâcle*. If, with the courage to look things in the face, we had that of suspending our course, if only for an instant, this respite, this pause on a global scale, would suffice to reveal to us the nature of the precipice over which we hang, and the resulting dread would quickly be converted into prayers or lamentations, into a salutary convulsion. But we cannot stop. And if the notion of the Inexorable seduces and supports us, it is because it contains, despite everything, a metaphysical residue, represents the only glimpse we still have of a sort of Absolute, without which nothing at all would subsist. Some day—who knows?—even this recourse may fail us. At the climax of our Void, we will be doomed, then, to the indignity of a complete erosion, worse than a sudden catastrophe which would be honorable after all, even glamorous. Let us be confident, let us put our bets on catastrophe, more in accord with our genius and our tastes. Let us take one step further, let us suppose it to be upon us, let us treat it as a *fait accompli.* According to all appearances, it will

include certain survivors, a few lucky ones who will
have had the good fortune to contemplate its occur-
rence and to draw lessons from it. Their first concern
will certainly be to abolish the memory of the old
humanity, of all the enterprises that have discredited
and destroyed it. Turning against the cities, they will
seek to complete their ruin, to erase all traces of them.
One rachitic tree will be worth more in their eyes than
a museum or a temple. No more schools; on the other
hand, courses in oblivion and unlearning to celebrate
the virtues of inattention and the delights of amnesia.
The disgust inspired by the sight of any book, frivolous or serious, will extend to all Knowledge, which
will be referred to with embarrassment or dread as if it
were an obscenity or a scourge. To bother with philosophy, to elaborate a system, to attach oneself to it and
believe in it, will appear as an impiety, a provocation,
and a betrayal, a criminal complicity with the past.
Tools, all execrated, will be used by no one, except
perhaps to sweep away the debris of a collapsed universe. Each will try to model himself upon the vegetable world, to the detriment of the animals, which will
be blamed for suggesting, in certain aspects, the figure
or the exploits of man; for the same reason, we shall
abstain from reviving the gods, and still less the idols.
So radical will be the rejection of history that it will be
condemned *en bloc*, without pity or nuance. And so it
shall be with time, identified with a blunder or with a
profligacy.

Recovering from the delirium of action, the

survivors, turning to monotony, will do their best to delight in it, to wallow there, in order to avoid the solicitations of the new. Each morning, contemplative and discreet, they will murmur certain anathemas against the previous generations; but among themselves, no suspect or sordid sentiment, no rancor or desire to humiliate or to eclipse anyone at all. Free and equal, they will nonetheless set above themselves anyone who, in his life or in his thought, retains none of the vices of engulfed humanity. All will venerate him and know no peace until they resemble him.

Let us leave off these divagations, for it serves no purpose to invent a "comforting interlude," wearisome feature of all eschatologies. Not that we may not conceive this new humanity, transfigured on the brink of the horrible; yet who can assure us that, its goal once achieved, it would not fall back into the miseries of the old one? And how are we to believe that it would not weary of bliss or that it would escape the lure of disaster, the temptation of playing, it too, a rôle? Boredom in the midst of paradise generated our first ancestor's appetite for the abyss which has won us this procession of centuries whose end we now have in view. That appetite, a veritable nostalgia for hell, would not fail to ravage the race following us and to make it the worthy heir of our misfortunes. Let us then renounce all prophecies, those frantic hypotheses, let us no longer allow ourselves to be deceived by the image of a remote and improbable future; let us abide by our certitudes, our indubitable abysses.

II

Stabs at Bewilderment

I ✒

"If we could teach geography to the carrier pigeon, its unconscious flight, which finds its goal straightway, would immediately become an impossibility." (Carl-Gustav Carus) [14] The writer who switches languages finds himself in the situation of this learned and crippled pigeon.

✒

Never try to make things easier for the reader. He will not thank you for your trouble. It is not understanding that he likes—he likes to mark time, to get stuck, he likes to be *punished*. Whence the prestige of certain murky authors; whence the perennial appeal of the hodgepodge.

✒

Léon Bloy [15] speaks of Pascal's *occult mediocrity*. The phrase strikes me as sacrilegious, and indeed it is,

64

though not absolutely, since Pascal, excessive in everything, was excessive in his common sense as well.

⚓

Philosophers write for professors; thinkers, for writers.

⚓

The Anatomy of Melancholy. —The best title ever invented. Unimportant if the book to which it is attached is more or less indigestible.

⚓

Perhaps we should publish only our first drafts, before we ourselves know what we are trying to say.

⚓

Only unfinished—because unfinishable—works prompt us to speculate about the essence of art.

⚓

What advantage would having faith be to me, since I understand Meister Eckhart [16] just as well without it?

✐

What cannot be translated into mystical language does not deserve to be experienced.

✐

To be related to that primordial Unity which the Rig-Veda[17] says "breathed of its own accord without drawing breath."

✐

Encounter with a subman. Three hours that might have turned to torment, had I not continuously reminded myself that I was not wasting my time, that after all I was lucky enough to contemplate a specimen of what humanity will be in a few generations . . .

✐

I have known no one who loved failure so much; and yet she killed herself to escape it.

✐

L. wants to know if I have a suicide line, but I hide my hands, and rather than show them to him, I shall always wear gloves in his presence.

✐

Stabs at Bewilderment

A book should open old wounds, even inflict new ones. A book should be a *danger*.

~

At the market, two old women gossip together, very seriously. At the moment of separation, one of them—the more deteriorated of the pair—concludes: "To have a little peace and quiet, you have to keep to what's normal in life." This, in virtually the same terms, is what Epictetus professed.

~

C. tells me about a visit to London, where in a hotel room, for an entire month, he remained motionless, *face to the wall*. For him, this was an exceptional happiness which he longed to extend indefinitely. I cite him an analogous experience, that of the Buddhist missionary Bodhidharma, which lasted for nine years . . .

Since I envy his prowess, which he does not boast about at all, I tell him that even if it remains his sole exploit, it should still gain him credit in his own eyes and help him to surmount the crises of prostration he cannot extricate himself from.

~

Paris wakes. On this November morning, it is still dark: on the Avenue de l'Observatoire, a bird—

just one—tries out its song. I stop and listen. All at once, growls and grunts in the vicinity. Impossible to know where they are coming from. Finally I catch a glimpse of two bums sleeping under a truck: one of them must be having a bad dream. The spell is broken. I clear out. In the Place Saint-Sulpice, in the urinal, I stumble over a half-naked little old woman . . . I utter a shriek of horror and dash into the church where a hunchbacked, squint-eyed priest is explaining to a dozen disinherited of all ages that the end of the world is at hand and that the punishment of the Last Judgment will be terrible.

*

Fortunate those who, born before Science, were privileged to die of their first disease!

*

To have introduced the sigh into the intellect's economy . . .

*

My disorders, my fatigues, my forced interest in physiology have led me to scorn all speculation as such. And if, during so many years, I have made no progress in any direction, at least I shall have learned what it is to have a *body*.

~

An old friend, a bum or, if you prefer, an itinerant musician, having returned to spend some time with his parents in the Ardennes, was provoked by some trifle to quarrel with his mother, a retired schoolteacher, just as she was getting ready to go to Mass. Beside herself, mute and pale, she flung down her hat, her coat, then her blouse, her skirt, her underwear and stockings, and stark naked performed a lascivious dance before her horrified husband and son pressed against the wall, incapable of stopping her with a gesture, a word. The performance over, she collapsed into a chair and burst into sobs.

~

On the wall, a print representing the execution of the Armagnac partisans, whose expression is a combination of derision, hilarity, and ecstasy. As if they feared nothing so much as seeing their torment come to an end . . .

The spectacle of such unspeakable and provocative bliss is one I can never get enough of.

~

Drawn and Quartered

Friendship being incompatible with truth, only the mute dialogue with our enemies is fruitful.

～

Those close to us must not die during one of our periods of atony. Otherwise, what an effort to bother with their misfortune!

～

"And the last shall be first"—It was at the Collège de France, on January 30, 1958, during Puech's lecture on the Gospel According to Thomas, that this refrain, uttered in the midst of an erudite commentary, plunged me into a strange condition. Had I heard it on my deathbed, it would not have moved me so much.

～

A Spanish poet sends me a greeting card showing a *rat*, the symbol, he writes, of all that we can "esperar" for the year to come. For every year, he might have added.

～

Whoever is crazy enough to embark on some work, whatever its nature, cannot tolerate, in his heart

of hearts, the slightest restriction as to what he is doing. His self-doubts undermine him too much for him
to confront those he inspires in others as well.

⚓

One of the Ancients said that the doctrine of
Epicurus had the "sweetness of the sirens." It would
be a waste of effort to look for a modern system that
would deserve such praise.

⚓

When I read Herodotus, I seem to hear some
Eastern peasant narrate and "philosophize." —Not for
nothing had he traveled among the Scythians.

⚓

Visit from a young man recommended by a
lady whose note described him as some kind of "genius." After having given me certain details about a
recent trip to Africa, he told me about his concerns,
his reading, his projects. In everything he said, there
was something wrong, a blank fever that made me
uncomfortable. Impossible to know who he was and
what he was worth. After an hour or so, he stood up,
as did I, he looked at me hard, and with an expression
at once concentrated and absent, walked toward me
slowly, very slowly, like a hallucinated snail. I remem-

ber thinking: "This genius is going to murder me," and stepped back, determined to punch him in the face if he came any closer. He stopped, made a nervous gesture, as if he were doing some violence to himself, as if—like another Dr. Jekyll—he were resisting some sinister metamorphosis, then grew calm, returned to his chair, struggling to smile again. I asked no question that might disturb him further. We resumed the conversation exactly where it had been broken off, and as he became himself again, I felt that *his* condition was taking *me* over, and that it was now my turn to stand up. At which point, luckily, it occurred to him to take his leave.

~

It is my elocutionary defects, my stammerings, my jerky delivery, my *art* of mumbling—it is my voice, my transeuropean *r*'s, that have impelled me by reaction to take some care with what I write and to make myself more or less worthy of an idiom I mistreat each time I open my mouth.

~

Among the miseries (old age, disease, etc.) that justify the search for deliverance, Buddha cites "stage fright"! In this regard, you would have to begin and end with the very human fear of being human.

Stabs at Bewilderment

This octogenarian confesses, under the seal of secrecy, that he has just experienced, for the first time in his life, the temptation to commit suicide. Why so much mystery? The shame of having waited so long to experience so legitimate a desire, or on the contrary, the horror of what he must regard as a monstrosity?

Pascal, alas, did not concern himself with suicide. Yet here was a subject to his hand. No doubt he would have been *against*, but with revealing concessions.

"A taste for the extraordinary is characteristic of mediocrity." (Diderot) . . . And we are still amazed that the Enlightenment had no understanding of Shakespeare.

One does not write because one has something to say but because one *wants* to say something.

Drawn and Quartered

If there is ever a moment when you must burst out laughing, it comes on those nights of intolerable discomfort, when you get up without knowing if you will write your last will or confine yourself to some wretched aphorism.

What is pain? A sensation reluctant to fade, an *ambitious* sensation.

Existing is plagiarism.

According to the Kabbalah, once a human being is conceived, he bears within his mother's womb a luminous sign which is extinguished at birth . . .

I would not want to live in a world drained of all religious feeling. I am not thinking of faith but of that inner vibration which, independent of any belief in particular, projects you into, and sometimes *above* God . . .

Stabs at Bewilderment

"No one has ever been able to free himself from Time." As I knew. But when I read it in the Mahâbhârata, then I know it forever.

If the narrative of the Fall is so striking, it is because its author describes neither entities nor symbols: he *sees* a God strolling in a garden, a *rural* God, as one exegete has so accurately characterized Him.

"Every time I think of Christ's crucifixion, I commit the sin of envy." —I love Simone Weil when she vies with the greatest saints for pride.

It is wrong to claim that man cannot live without gods. At first he needs to create false gods, but later on he endures everything, accustoms himself to everything. He is not noble enough to perish out of disappointment.

Drawn and Quartered

In this dream, I was flattering someone I despise. Waking, a greater self-loathing than if I had really committed such a vileness . . .

⇥

I feel effective, competent, likely to do something positive only when I lie down and abandon myself to an interrogation without object or end.

⇥

Sterility makes us lucid and pitiless. Once we cease producing, we find what others do to be without inspiration and without substance. Doubtless a true judgment. But we should have extended it, when we were producing, when in fact we were doing what others do.

⇥

True moral elegance consists in the art of disguising one's victories as defeats.

⇥

Those unsuccessful nightmares, the ones that linger, that continue for lack of new catastrophes . . . To wake up with a start out of boredom!

Stabs at Bewilderment

Death is a state of perfection, the only one within a mortal's grasp.

In the days when I smoked all the time, a cigarette, after a sleepless night, had a funereal taste which consoled me for everything.

In this suburban train, a little girl (five years old?) is reading a picture book. She comes to the word "passage" and asks her mother what it means. "Passage—the train passes, or a man passes in the street, the wind passes . . ." The child, who looks quite bright, does not seem satisfied with the answer. Doubtless she finds the examples too *concrete*.

That day, we happened to be discussing "theology" at table. The housemaid, an illiterate peasant woman, was listening where she stood. "I only believe in God when I have a toothache," she said. After a whole life, her remark is the only one I remember.

Drawn and Quartered

⇥

In an English magazine, a diatribe against Marcus Aurelius, whom the author accuses of hypocrisy, philistinism, and posturing. Furious, I was on the verge of writing a reply when, thinking of the Emperor, I quickly got hold of myself. It was only fair that I should not yield to anger in the name of one who taught me never to yield to anger.

⇥

Each concession we make is accompanied by an inner diminution of which we are not immediately conscious.

⇥

To that friend who tells me he is bored because he cannot work, I answer that boredom is a *higher* state, and that we debase it by relating it to the notion of work.

⇥

To exist is a colossal phenomenon—*which has no meaning.* This is how I should define the stupefaction in which I live day after day.

⇥

Stabs at Bewilderment

You told me that I was worthless when I affirmed that I was of some avail only when I doubted. But I am not a doubter, I am an idolater of doubt, a doubter in eruption, a fanatic without creed, a hero of fluctuation.

Oedipus and his inquiry, the relentless pursuit of truth, without consideration and without scruple, the determination upon his own ruin, reminds us of the progress and the mechanism of Knowledge, an activity eminently incompatible with the instinct of self-preservation.

To be *convinced* of anything is an unheard-of exploit, almost miraculous . . .

We must censure the later Nietzsche for a panting excess in the writing, the absence of *rests*.

The only words that count, that are contagious, are those resulting from illumination or from frenzy, two states in which one is *unrecognizable*.

79

Drawn and Quartered

Christ, it has been argued, was not a sage—
witness his words on the occasion of the Last Supper:
"This do in remembrance of me." Now the sage never
speaks in his own name: the sage is impersonal.
Granted. But Christ made no claim to be a sage. He
had taken himself for a god, and that required a language less modest, a personal language, precisely.

One struggles, one labors, one sacrifices, apparently for oneself, actually for anyone at all, for
some future enemy, for an unknown enemy. And this
is even truer of peoples than of individuals. Heraclitus
was mistaken: it is not the lightning, but irony that
rules the universe. It is irony that is the law of the
world.

Even when nothing happens, everything seems
too much to me. What can be said, then, in the presence of an event, of any event?

The greatest of follies is to believe that we walk
on solid ground. Once history calls attention to its

existence, we are convinced of the contrary. Our steps seem to adhere to the earth, and we suddenly discover that there is no such thing as ground, that there is also no such thing as steps.

≁

At the Zoo. —All these creatures have a decent bearing, except the monkeys. One feels that man is not far off.

≁

In Dangeau's[18] *Journal* we can read: "Mme la Duchesse d'Harcourt requests and obtains the inheritance of one Foucault who has killed himself." —"Today the king has given to the Dauphine a man who has killed himself. She expects to gain a great deal of money thereby."

Remember this when tempted to excuse the age of perruques and to wonder at the guillotine.

≁

Impossible to accede to truth by opinions, for each opinion is only a *mad* perspective of reality.

≁

According to one Hindu legend, Shiva, at a particular moment, will begin to dance, at first slowly, then faster and faster, and will not stop before having imposed upon the world a frenzied cadence, in every respect opposed to that of Creation.

This legend includes no commentary, history having assumed the task of illustrating its obvious truth.

⚓

While they were preparing the hemlock, Socrates was learning how to play a new tune on the flute. "What will be the use of that?" he was asked. "To know this tune before dying."

If I dare repeat this reply long since trivialized by the handbooks, it is because it seems to me the sole serious justification of any desire to know, whether exercised on the brink of death or at any other moment of existence.

⚓

According to Origen,[19] only the souls given to evil, "their wings broken," don bodies again. In other words, without a wicked appetite, no incarnation, no history. This terrifying evidence becomes tolerable once we surround it with the barest theological apparatus.

⚓

Stabs at Bewilderment

The true Messiah will appear, we are told, only in a world "entirely just" or "entirely culpable." The second eventuality alone deserving consideration, since it is almost in range and since it agrees so well with what we *know* of the future, the Messiah has every likelihood of appearing at last and responding not so much to an old hope as to an old fear.

〜

I have often noted that it is easier to go back to sleep after a dream in which we are murdered than after a dream in which we are the murderer. A good mark for the murderer.

〜

At Saint-Séverin, an Italian choir sings Cavalieri's *Lamentations of Jeremiah*. At the climax of emotion, I remind myself to settle acounts with . . . In the most "ethereal" moments, I am invariably seized by the desire to take immediate revenge for an injury in no way recent but maybe ten, twenty, thirty years old.

〜

There is no one whose death I have not longed for, at one moment or another.

❧

D., a good psychologist despite his senility, clung to his discoveries. Each time I ran into him, he would tell me that my rages made him think of King Lear's, whose threats he immediately recited:

> *"I will do such things—*
> *What they are, yet I know not, but they shall be*
> *The terrors of the earth."*

Whereupon the little old fellow laughed like a child.

❧

According to an Hassidic text, he who does not find the true way, or who leaves it deliberately, comes to the point of living solely by "diabolic pride." Who could help feeling accused here!

❧

Eternity: I wonder how, without losing my reason, I can have uttered this word so many times.

❧

"And I saw the dead, small and great, stand before God." *Small and great!* surely an involuntary touch of humor. Even in the Apocalypse, trifles count, indeed it is they which constitute its attraction.

⟡

Death, what a dishonor! To become suddenly an *object* . . .

⟡

To detest someone is to want him to be anything but what he is. T. writes me that I am the man he loves most in the world . . . but he urges me at the same time to forgo my obsessions, to change my ways, to become different, to break with the man I am. Which is to say that he rejects my *being*.

⟡

Detachment, serenity—vague, almost empty words, except in those moments when we would have answered by a smile if we had been told we had only a few minutes left to live.

⟡

Out of therapeutic concern, he had put into his books everything in himself that was impure, the residue of his thought, the dregs of his mind.

Drawn and Quartered

⚓

Of all that is supposed to belong to the realm of the "psychic," nothing is so physiological as depression, active in the tissues, the blood, the bones, in any organ taken separately. Left to its own devices, depression would demolish even the fingernails.

⚓

Musical Offering, Art of the Fugue, Goldberg Variations: I love in music, as in philosophy and in everything, what pains by insistence, by recurrence, by that interminable return which reaches the ultimate depths of being and provokes there a barely endurable delectation.

⚓

What a pity that "nothingness" has been devalued by an abuse of it made by philosophers unworthy of it!

⚓

When we have laid claim to a monopoly of disappointment, we must do ourselves violence in order to admit that someone else is entitled to be disappointed.

⚓

Nothing makes us modest, not even the sight of a corpse.

~

Every act of courage is the work of an unbalanced man. Animals, normal by definition, are always cowardly except when they *know themselves* to be stronger, which is cowardice itself.

~

If everything were tending toward the best, the old, furious at being unable to take advantage of this situation, would all die of vexation. Fortunately for them, the course history has taken from the start is reassuring—it permits them to perish without the slightest trace of jealousy.

~

Whoever speaks the language of utopia is more alien to me than a reptile from another geological era.

~

The only time we can be content with ourselves is when, according to a Japanese phrase, we remember having perceived the *Ah!* of things.

Drawn and Quartered

✦

Illusion begets and sustains the world; we do not destroy one without destroying the other. Which is what I do every day. An apparently ineffectual operation, since I must begin all over again the next day.

✦

Time is corroded from within, exactly like an organism, like everything that is stricken with life. To say *Time* is to say *lesion,* and what a lesion!

✦

I realized I had grown old when I began feeling that the word Destruction had lost its power, that it no longer gave me that thrill of triumph and plenitude allied to prayer, an aggressive prayer . . .

✦

No sooner had I completed a series of rather lugubrious reflexions than I was gripped by that morbid love of life, punishment or reward for none but those dedicated to negation.

II ✐

I once maintained I could honor only a man who is dishonored and happy. I have just realized that Epictetus[20] went further: *dying* and *happy*, he said. Yet perhaps it is easier to exult in the last agony than in ignominy.

✐

The idea of the Eternal Return can be fully grasped only by a man endowed with several chronic, hence recurrent infirmities, and who thus has the advantage of proceeding from relapse to relapse, with all that this implies as philosophic reflexion.

✐

A self-respecting man is a man without a country. A fatherland is birdlime . . .

89

Drawn and Quartered

⚮

A medical bookstore. In the window, right up front, a skeleton. I spat with disgust. Afterward, I reminded myself that I should have evinced a little gratitude, seeing how many times I have celebrated those sardonic bones, whose idea, if not whose image, has so charitably sustained me on so many occasions.

⚮

To send someone a book is to commit a burglary—a case of breaking and entering. It is to trample down his solitude, what he holds most sacred, for it is to oblige him to desist from himself in order to think about your thoughts.

⚮

At C.'s burial, I was reminding myself: "Here at last was someone who didn't have a single enemy." This was not because he was mediocre, but because he was unprecedentedly ignorant of the *intoxication of wounding*.

⚮

X. no longer knows what to do with himself. Events trouble him to excess. His panic is salutary to me: it forces me to calm him, and this effort of persuasion, this search for soothing arguments, soothes me in my turn. In order to keep on this side of madness, you must frequent those more demented than yourself.

✦

All these hard, forbidding eyes. In case of a riot, one dares not imagine their expression. The word "neighbor" has no meaning in big cities. It was a term legitimate in rural civilizations, where people knew each other at sight, and could enjoy or detest one another in peace.

✦

A Tantric ritual: during the initiation ceremony, you are given a mirror in which you see your own image. Contemplating it, you realize you are nothing but that, *i.e.*, nothing.

To what end, so many pretenses, so many airs and graces, when it is so easy to comprehend one's insignificance?

✦

Plotinus experienced only four moments of ecstasy; Ramana Maharshi, but one. What does the number matter!

If anyone is to be pitied, it is the man who has

never had even an inkling of such things, and who speaks of them from hearsay.

~

This little blind creature, only a few days old, turning its head every which way in search of something or other, this naked skull, this initial baldness, this tiny monkey that has sojourned for months in a latrine and that soon, forgetting its origins, will spit on the galaxies . . .

~

In almost all thinkers, we may discern the need to *believe* in the subjects they discuss—they even identify themselves with these subjects to a certain point. This need, blameworthy in theory, nonetheless turns out to be a blessing, since because of it they are not disgusted with thinking itself . . .

~

If there were a common, even official form of killing oneself, suicide would be much easier and much more frequent. But since to be done with it all we must find our own way, we waste so much time meditating on trifles that we forget what is essential.

~

Stabs at Bewilderment

For a few minutes I have concentrated on the *passage* of time, my entire attention fastened to the emergence and disappearance of each instant. In truth, my mind was not fixed upon the individual instant (which does not exist), but on the phenomenon of the passage itself, on the interminable disaggregation of the present. Were we to make this experiment without interruption for a whole day, our brain too would disintegrate.

~

To be is to be cornered.

~

In flawed families, a scion appears who dedicates himself to the truth and who ruins himself in its pursuit.

~

What has most amazed me in most of the philosophers I have been able to approach is their lack of judgment. Invariably they *miss* . . . A remarkable incapacity for accuracy. —The habit of abstraction dulls the wits.

~

In the last, say, forty years, not a day has passed when I haven't had something like an *undeclared* epileptic fit. This is what has allowed me to keep in shape and to save appearances.

... *What appearances?*

✍

Natures capable of objectivity in any and every situation give the impression of abnormality. What has been broken or perverted in them? Impossible to know, but one divines some serious problem, some anomaly. Impartiality is incompatible with the will to affirm oneself or quite simply with the will to exist. To acknowledge another's merits is an alarming symptom, an act against nature.

✍

"Neither this world, nor the next, nor happiness are for the being abandoned to doubt."

This point in the Gita is my death sentence.

✍

I try to oppose the interest I take in her, I imagine her eyes, her cheeks, her nose, her lips in a high state of putrefaction. No help for it: the indefinable element she releases persists. It is in such moments that one understands why life has managed to sustain itself, in spite of Knowledge.

Once one has understood, it would be best to drop dead on the spot. What is *to understand?* What we have really grasped cannot be expressed in any way at all, and cannot be transmitted to anyone else, not even to oneself, so that we die without knowing the exact nature of our own secret.

Not to think about anything except what you would like to ponder in a grave.

I have always been attracted by lost causes, by individuals without a hope of success, whose follies I have espoused until I suffer from them almost as much as they do. When you are committed to tormenting yourself, your own torments, however enormous, are not enough; you fling yourself on those of others as well, you appropriate them, you make yourself doubly, trebly—what am I saying? a hundredfold miserable.

Drawn and Quartered

To have the sense of the *perpetual* only in the negative, in what does harm, in what thwarts being. Perpetuity of threat, of frustration, of longed-for and failed ecstasy, of an absolute glimpsed and rarely achieved; yet sometimes transcended, skipped over, as when you escape God . . .

At the edge of the woods, a wounded ringdove. A stray bullet must have grazed it. It could escape only by hopping along. Its comical movements, *that seemed to amuse it*, gave its agony a cheerful character. I had an impulse to pick it up, for the air was cold and night was coming on. But I had no idea whom to entrust it to: no one would have had any use for it in this gloomy and forbidding Beauce. I could hardly try playing on the sympathies of the railroad official in the little station where I was about to take a train. And so I abandoned the bird to its *joy* of dying.

To have been forever tormented by eminently loyal ailments and to manage to convince no one of their reality. Yet on thinking it over, this is only fair: one does not wield with impunity, in company, the talents of a chatterbox and the life of the party. How, later on, to persuade others of the existence of a *cheerful* martyr?

*

To be weary not only of what you have desired but even of what you *could* have desired! Indeed, of any possible desire.

*

The superior saints did not insist on working miracles; they acknowledged them reluctantly, as if *someone* had forced their hand. So strong a repugnance for such things doubtless came to them from the fear of falling into the sin of pride and of yielding to the temptation of Titanism, the desire to equal God and to steal His powers.

Sometimes, in the will's paroxysms, you realize you can *force* the laws of nature. These moments are so exhausting that they leave you panting, stripped of that inner energy which might encroach upon and overturn these laws. If merely the *intention* to work a miracle exhausts, what would be the case with the miracle itself?

*

Drawn and Quartered

Every time we come upon something existing, real, full, we want to have the bells rung, as on the occasion of great victories or great calamities.

⤚

To experience, in a marketplace, sensations the Desert Fathers would have envied.

⤚

I want to proclaim a truth that would forever exile me from among the living. I know only the conditions but not the words that would allow me to formulate it.

⤚

You have dared call Time your "brother," take as your ally the worst of torturers. On this point, our differences explode: you walk in step with Time, while I precede or drag after it, never adopting its manners, unable to think of it without experiencing something like a *speculative sorrow.*

⤚

According to a Gnostic Revelation, we fall short of the Most High when we call Him *infinite,* for He is, it is said, *much more than that.*

I should like to know the name of this author who has so remarkably seen the nature of God's extravagant singularity.

～

A pity we can make no progress in modesty! I have applied myself to doing so with no little zeal, but have succeeded only in moments of extreme lassitude. Lassitude gone, my efforts turn out to be futile. Modesty must be anything but a natural condition if we attain it only by means of exhaustion.

～

That shipwrecked man who, washed ashore on an island and immediately noticing a gallows, instead of being alarmed was reassured: he had landed among savages, of course, but in a place where order reigned.

～

I think more than I should of the emotions of a pagan after Constantine's conversion. I spend my life in perpetual fear of dogmas, of dawning dogmas.

Declining dogmas, on the other hand, delight me, for they have lost their aggressiveness. Yet knowing them to be threatened, I cannot forget that it is their deliquescence which is preparing the advent of a world I dread. And the sympathy they inspire in me ends by feeding my terror . . .

Success, honors, and all the rest of it are pardonable only if he who experiences them *feels* that he will end badly. Then he will accept them solely in order to enjoy, when the moment comes, the completeness of his collapse.

"I have seen nothing so impassive in the icy marble of statues," Barras writes of Robespierre. —I wonder if the imperturbability of Talleyrand's proud profligacy was not an ultrarefined copy of the style of the Incorruptible . . .

To found a family. I think it would have been easier for me to found an empire.

The real writer writes about beings, things, events, he does not write about writing, he uses words but does not linger over them, making them the object of his ruminations. He will be anything and every-thing except an anatomist of the Word. Dissection of language is the fad of those who, having nothing to say, confine themselves to the saying.

☞

After suffering a serious illness, in certain Asian countries—in Laos, for example—one tradition-ally changes one's name. What a vision lies at the ori-gin of such a custom! Actually we should change our name after each important experience.

☞

Only a flower that falls is a complete flower, say the Japanese. One is tempted to say as much of a civilization.

☞

The basis of society, of any society, is a certain *pride in obedience*. When this pride no longer exists, the society collapses.

☞

My passion for history derives from my nose for the decrepit and my appetite for the *squandered*.

101

Are you a reactionary? —If you say so, but in the same sense that God is . . .

One is and remains a slave as long as one is not *cured* of hoping.

Comforting to be able to tell oneself: my life corresponds feature for feature to the kind of slough I always wanted.

For thirty years, my father administered extreme unction thousands of times. No more than the gravedigger, his "companion," did he have the sentiment of death, a sentiment that has nothing to do with the *corpse*, an intimate sentiment, the most intimate of all, and which you would feel, if you are predestined to feel it, even in a world where no one has occasion to die.

Those moments when you behave as if nothing had ever been, when all expectation is suspended for lack of *instants*, and when, in the depths of yourself, you would be utterly lost to find the slightest fragment of being still sullied by the Possible . . .

This nonagenarian passes away without being sick—nothing wrong with her, she is dying only because she can last no longer . . . Going to her house, I found her half-unconscious. She had the strength to murmur: "It's the end of life, it's the end of life."—"All the same, you shouldn't care," I answered. She smiled uncertainly, perhaps scornfully. I must have seemed either too naïve or too cynical, or both at once.

When I see someone fighting for some cause or other, I try to know what is happening in his mind and what can be the source of his obvious lack of maturity. The rejection of resignation is perhaps a sign of "life," never in any case of perspicacity or simply of reflexion. The sane man never lowers himself to *protest*. He scarcely consents to indignation. Taking human affairs seriously attests to some secret flaw.

An anthropologist who had gone to study the Pygmies reported with amazement that the tribes living in the vicinity regarded him with contempt and kept him at a distance because he frequented an inferior tribe, the Pygmies being in their eyes people of no merit, "dogs," unworthy of waking the least interest.

Nothing is more exclusivist than a vigorous, unbroken instinct. A community consolidates itself insofar as it is inhuman, as it can exclude . . . The "primitives" excel in this. Not they but the "civilized" have invented tolerance, and it will be the death of us. Why have we invented it? Because we were in the process of dying . . . It is not tolerance that has weakened us, it is our weakness, our deficient vitality which has made us tolerant.

*

The two women I have most frequented: Theresa of Avila and the Marquise de Brinvilliers.[21]

*

Those obsessed with the worst—we resent them even as we acknowledge the accuracy of their apprehensions and admonitions. We are much more indulgent to those who have been mistaken because we suppose that their blindness was the fruit of enthusiasm and generosity, whereas the others, prisoners of their lucidity, would be only cowards, incapable of assuming the risk of an illusion.

꒯

All things considered, the age of the cavemen was not the ideal. The epoch immediately following, yes, when after such a long claustration, man could finally think *outside* . . .

꒯

I do not struggle against the world, I struggle against a greater force, against my *weariness* of the world.

꒯

This old sexuality is *something*, all the same . . . Ever since life has been life, we were right, it must be said, to make so much of it. How else account for the fact that we grow tired of everything, except of it? The oldest exercise of the living cannot fail to mark us, and we realize that he who has no dealing with it is a being apart—an outcast or a saint.

꒯

The more injustices one has suffered, the more one risks yielding to infatuation or, quite simply, to pride. Every victim flatters himself that he is Chosen in reverse and reacts in consequence, without suspecting that he thereby attains to the status of the Devil himself.

~

As soon as one returns to Doubt (if it could be said that one has ever left it), undertaking anything at all seems not so much useless as extravagant. No joyful companion, Doubt works deep within you like a disease or, even more effectively, like a faith.

~

Tacitus has Otho, determined to kill himself but convinced by his soldiers to postpone his action, say: "Very well, let us add one more night to our life."
. . . Let us hope for Otho that his night did not resemble the one I have just spent.

~

According to the Talmud, the bad impulse is innate, the good appears only at the age of thirteen . . . This specificity, despite its comical character, possesses a certain verisimilitude and reveals the incurable timidity of the Good, in the face of Evil so comfortably installed in our substance and enjoying

there privileges which grant its quality of prior oc-
cupancy.

⚞

The Messiah, for the Jews, could only be a tri-
umphant king; in no case, a victim. Too ambitious to
be content with a crucified man, they were waiting for
someone *strong.* Their luck was not to realize that Jesus
was strong *in his way.* Otherwise they would have
joined the Christian hordes and, lamentably, vanished
forever.

⚞

Our infirmities keep us from escaping ourselves, from becoming different, from changing our
skin, from being capable of metamorphosis. After
each step forward, they make us take one step back, so
that we can make no progress except in the knowledge
of our useless identity.

⚞

My mission is to kill time, and time's is to kill
me in its turn. How comfortable one is among mur-
derers.

⚞

Drawn and Quartered

The obsession of *lastness* apropos of every-thing, *the last* as category, as constitutive form of the mind, as original deformity, even as revelation . . .

✍

On my desk for months now, a huge hammer: a symbol of what? I don't know, but its presence is beneficial to me and at moments gives me that as-surance which must be familiar to all who take shelter behind some certainty or other.

✍

Abruptly, a need to testify to the recognition not only of beings but of objects, to a stone because it is a stone . . . How alive everything becomes! As if for eternity. Suddenly, *nonexistence* seems inconceivable. That such impulses appear, *can* appear, shows that the last word may not reside in Negation.

✍

Visit from a painter who describes how, calling one evening on a blind man and finding him alone in the dark, he could not keep from pitying him and asking him if existence was endurable without light. *"You don't know what you're missing,"* was the blind man's answer.

Stabs at Bewilderment

＊

These fits of rage, this need to explode, to spit in everyone's face, to slap one universe after the next—how to vanquish them? It would take a little turn in a cemetery, or better still, a *definitive* turn . . .

＊

Not a day, not an hour, not even a minute without falling into what Shandrakirti, the Buddhist dialectician, calls the *"abyss of the heresy of self."*

＊

Among the Iroquois, when an old man could no longer hunt, his family offered to abandon him in the wilderness, letting him starve to death, or else to break open his head with a tomahawk. The subject of this concern almost invariably opted for the latter formula. An important detail: before facing him with this choice, the entire family sang the *Song of the Great Remedy.*

What "advanced" society has ever given proof of so much good sense, so much humor?

＊

I long ago used up whatever religious resources I had. Desiccation or purification? I am the last to say. No god lingers in my blood . . .

⚰

Never lose sight of the fact that the plebs regretted Nero. This is what we must remember whenever we are tempted by whatever chimera may attack us . . .

⚰

To think that for such a long time I have done nothing but concern myself with my corpse, busied myself tinkering with it instead of throwing it on the dungheap, for the greatest good of both!

⚰

I have less and less discernment as to what is good and what evil. When I make no distinction whatever between the two, supposing I reach this point some day—what a step forward! Toward what?

⚰

How fitting seems that notion of the Kabbalah, according to which the brain, the eyes, the ears, the hands and even the feet have a distinct soul which is theirs alone! Such souls would be "sparks" of Adam ... What seems less obvious ...

⟆

Coming down the stairs, I hear on the floor above that apparently robust octogenarian singing thunderously: *Miserere nobis.* Half an hour later I'm coming back up and again I hear the same *"miserere,"* as urgent as before. —The first time, I managed to smile. The second, I had a kind of seizure.

⟆

That peace from beyond the grave that you feel when you abstract yourself from the world. I suddenly thought I could perceive a smile enclosing space itself. Who was smiling? From whom emanated this great happiness which submerges the faces of mummies? In one second I had gone over to the *other side*, in another I had to come back, quite unworthy to share the secret of the dead for a longer interval.

⟆

I have not experienced, strictly speaking, indigence. On the other hand, I have experienced if not

111

disease, at least *the absence of health,* which delivers me from remorse for not having lived in utter poverty.

⚘

How can you know if you are *in the truth?* The criterion is simple enough: if others make a vacuum around you, there is not a doubt in the world that you are closer to the essential than they.

⚘

Get hold of yourself, be confident once more, don't forget that it is not given to just anyone to have idolized discouragement without succumbing to it.

⚘

At the bird market. What power, what determination in these tiny frantic bodies! Life resides in this bit of nothing which animates a tuft of matter, and which nonetheless emerges from matter itself and perishes with it. But the perplexity remains: impossible to explain this fever, this perpetual dance, this representation, this spectacle which life affords itself. What a theater, breath!

⚘

All these people in the street make me think of exhausted gorillas, every one of them tired of imitating man!

If there existed some trace of a providential order, each of us would know exactly when he had done his time and would disappear forthwith. Since in such matters there is always a *for* and an *against*, we wait, we argue with ourselves, and the hours pass, and the days, in interrogation and indignity.

Within a perfect society, each of us would be told to vacate the premises as soon as he began to live beyond his time. Age would not always be the criterion, so many of the young being indistinguishable from ghosts. The whole question would be how to choose those whose mission would consist in deciding on our last hour.

If one managed to be *conscious* of the organs, of *all* the organs, one would have an experience and an absolute vision of one's own body, which would then be so present to consciousness that it could no longer perform the tasks to which it is assigned: it would itself become consciousness, and thereby would cease to perform its part as a body . . .

I have never stopped accusing my fate, for otherwise how would I have confronted it? To indict it was my only hope of accommodating myself to it and of enduring it. Hence I must continue to assail it—out of an instinct of self-preservation and by calculation, by egoism, in short.

A young man and a young woman, both mutes, speaking to one another by gestures. How happy they both looked!

All the evidence suggests that speech is not, and cannot be, the vehicle of happiness.

The further one advances into age, the more one runs after honors. Perhaps, in fact, vanity is never more active than on the brink of the grave. One clings to trifles in order not to realize what they conceal, one deceives nothingness by something even more null and void.

The state of health is a state of nonsensation, even of nonreality. As soon as we cease to suffer, we cease to exist.

✐

Madness does not smother envy, or even calm it. Witness X, who leaves his padded cell more poisonous than ever. If the straitjacket fails to modify a man's depths, what hope is there in a cure, or even in old age itself? After all, dementia is a shock more radical than dotage; and as we see, it seems to be of no help whatever.

✐

Knowing what I know, I should no longer run the risk of the slightest surprise. Yet the danger exists—indeed, it is an everyday affair. Such is my weakness. What shame, in truth, still to be able to be gratified, or disappointed!

✐

Dying is a superiority few seek out. As I reminded myself listening to this old man who is afraid of death, who thinks of it unceasingly. What would he not give to elude it! With a laughable desperation, he tries to convince me that it is inevitable . . . As he imagines it to himself, death seems even more certain than it is in reality. Without problems of health despite his age, without material worries, without attachments of any kind, he keeps chewing the cud of the same terror, whereas he could easily enjoy the time he has left . . . But no, "nature" has inflicted this torment in order to punish him for having escaped the others.

Plenitude as an ecstatic happiness is possible only in the moments when we become deeply conscious of the unreality of both life and death. These moments are rare as experiences, though they can be frequent in the order of reflexion. In this realm, only what we feel exists. Now, an unreality felt and yet transcended within one and the same action is a performance, a feat that rivals and sometimes eclipses ecstasy.

III ↝

Hesiod: "The gods have hidden from men the sources of life." Have they done well, or ill? One thing is certain: mortals would not have had the courage to continue after such a revelation.

↝

When we know what words are worth, the amazing thing is that we try to say anything at all, and that we manage to do so. This requires, it is true, a supernatural nerve.

↝

X informs me he would like to meet me. I accept eagerly. The closer the hour of our meeting comes, the more vigorously certain homicidal instincts awaken within me. Conclusion: never consent

117

to anything if you want to have a good opinion of yourself.

↬

I spend my time advising suicide in what I write and advising against it in what I say. This is because the first case concerns a philosophical issue; the second, a being, a voice, a complaint . . .

↬

In the Benares sermon, Buddha cites, among the causes of pain, the thirst to become and the thirst not to become. The first thirst we understand, but why the second? To long for nonbecoming—is that not to be released? What is meant here is not the goal but the way as such, the pursuit and the attachment to the pursuit. —Unfortunately, on the way to deliverance only the way is *interesting*. Deliverance? One does not attain it, one is engulfed in it, smothered in it. Nirvana itself—an asphyxia! Though the gentlest of all.

↬

Lacking the good luck to be a monster, in any realm whatever, including sanctity, you will inspire envy and scorn.

Stabs at Bewilderment

If a man displays an infirmity long enough, he cannot be taken for a malingerer. In a sense, he has *realized* himself. Every disease is an identification.

Whatever is exempt from the funereal is necessarily vulgar.

Strindberg, toward the end of his life, took the Luxembourg gardens for his Gethsemane. I too have known a kind of Calvary there—drawn out, it is true, over some forty years!

As soon as we consult a specialist, we realize we are the lowest of the low, the reject of Creation, a crud. We should not know *what* ails us, still less what we die of. Any specification in this realm is impious, for *by a word* it does away with that minimum of mystery which death and even life are meant to conceal.

Drawn and Quartered

To be a Barbarian and to be able to live only in a hothouse!

⚮

Suffering, even as it undermines our strength, augments our pride. Our enemy assumes our defense.

⚮

A prayer without constraint, a destructive, pulverizing prayer, a prayer irradiating the End!

⚮

In my fits of optimism, I remind myself that my life has been a hell, *my* hell, a hell to my taste.

⚮

Not that I lack air, no, but I don't know what to do with the air I have, I don't see why I should breathe . . .

⚮

Since death is the very realization of equilibrium, *life* and *disequilibrium* are indistinguishable: a unique example of perfect synonyms.

120

Stabs at Bewilderment

All my ideas come down to various discomforts debased into generalities.

Fever inspires a man's work—for how long? Often passion causes certain works to date, whereas others, produced by exhaustion, survive age after age. Timeless lassitude, eternity of cold disgust!

At the Spanish border, a few hundred tourists, most of them Scandinavian, were waiting at the customs office. A telegram is delivered to a heavyset, obviously Spanish woman. Opening it, she discovers that her mother has died, and utters a succession of groans. What a godsend, I was thinking, to be able to release one's grief on the spot instead of concealing it, accumulating it, as any of these palefaces would do, staring in embarrassment and victimized by their discretion, their restraint, until one of these days they will spend all they have at the psychoanalyst's.

The best means of consoling an unhappy man is to assure him that an incontestable curse weighs

121

upon him. This kind of flattery helps him endure his ordeals, the notion of malediction implying election, an elite kind of wretchedness. Even in the agony of death, a compliment works: pride vanishes only with consciousness and even occasionally survives it, as happens in our dreams where an adulation can function so intensely that it suddenly wakens us, leaving us ecstatic and ashamed.

The proof that man loathes man? Enough to be in a crowd, in order to feel that you side with all the dead planets.

By what aberration has suicide, the only truly normal action, become the attribute of the flawed?

. . . better be with the dead . . .
Than on the torture of the mind to lie
In restless ecstasy.

Thus Macbeth—my brother, my spokesman, my messenger, my alter ego.

—

To discern in the depths of oneself a bad principle that is not powerful enough to show itself in
daylight or weak enough to keep still, a kind of insom-
niac demon, obsessed by all the evil it has dreamed of,
by all the horrors it has not perpetrated . . .

—

There is no one who does not disparage him. I
defend him against everyone, I refuse to deliver a
moral judgment upon someone who, as a youth, having been called upon to identify his father's body in
the morgue, managed to deceive the watchman's vigilance and to remain there all night long. Such an exploit entitles a man to everything, and it is natural that
he should have felt it to do so.

—

"I shall take the liberty of praying for you."—
"Glad to hear it. But *who* will listen to you?"

—

We shall never know if, in what he writes
about Suffering, this philosopher is dealing with a

123

question of syntax or with the first and queen of sensations.

⊨

The only profitable conversations are with enthusiasts who have ceased being so—with the ex-naïve . . . Calmed down at last, they have taken, willy-nilly, the decisive step toward Knowledge—that impersonal version of disappointment.

⊨

To try curing someone of a "vice," of what is the deepest thing he has, is to attack his very being, and indeed this is how he himself understands it, since he will never forgive you for wanting him to destroy himself *in your way* and not in his.

⊨

It is not the instinct of self-preservation that keeps us going, it is only the impossibility of our *seeing* the future. Of seeing it? of merely imagining it. If we knew all that lies ahead of us, no one would stoop to persist. Since every future disaster remains abstract, we cannot absorb it. Moreover, we do not even absorb it when it falls upon us and *replaces* us.

⚓

What madness, to be concerned with history! —But what else can you do when you have been *transfixed* by Time?

⚓

I am interested in anyone, except *other people*. I could have been anything, except a legislator.

⚓

The phenomenon of being misunderstood or scorned is allied to an undeniable pleasure known to all whose work has never wakened a response. This kind of satisfaction, tinged with arrogance, tends to erode itself, for in time everything is jeopardized, including one's excessive notions about oneself, a factor of all ambition as of all work, whether enduring or botched.

⚓

He who, having frequented men, retains the slightest illusion about them, should be condemned to reincarnation, in order to learn how to observe, to see, to catch up . . .

⚓

125

The apparition of life? A temporary madness, a prank, a whim of the elements, a vagary of matter. The only ones entitled to grumble are the individual beings, pitiable victims of a passing fancy.

~

In a book of Oriental inspiration, the author suggests that he is filled, that he is "saturated with serenity." —He does not inform us clearly, the dear fellow, how he has gone about it, and we readily understand why.

~

The living—reprobates all, but unaware of the fact. I know it, but does that get me any further? Yes, it does—I *believe* I suffer more than they do.

"Save me from this passing hour" cries the *Imitation*. "Save me from every hour" would have been more accurate.

~

X is the man whose defects I have studied for years in order to improve myself . . . He granted importance to everything; I realized this was the one thing *not* to do. With his example ever present to my mind, how many enthusiasms I have been freed from!

126

Stabs at Bewilderment

Amazing, that passage where Jacqueline Pascal, sister of the philosopher, praises her brother's progress in the "desire to be annihilated in the esteem and memory of men." This is the way I had hoped to take, which I *have* taken on occasion, but on which I must have bogged down . . .

During bad nights, there comes a moment when you stop struggling, when you lay down your arms: a peace follows, an invisible triumph, the supreme reward after the pangs which have preceded it. *To accept* is the secret of limits. Nothing equals a fighter who renounces, nothing rivals the ecstasy of capitulation . . .

According to Nagarjuna—a subtle mind, if ever there was one, and who transcended even nihilism— Buddha offered the world the "nectar of vacuity." At the limits of the most abstract and the most destructive analysis, to evoke a draught, even of the gods—is this not a weakness, a concession? —However far one may have advanced, one still drags along the indignity of being—or of having been—human.

Drawn and Quartered

At that noisy dinner, we talked of one thing and another. Suddenly X's smiling portrait attracted my attention. How pleased he seemed, and what a light shone from his countenance! Always happy, even in paint! And then I began envying him, and resenting him, as if he had stolen some of my opportunities. And then came a relief, a sudden comfort, remembering that he was dead.

More and more, I tend to side with Epicurus when he mocks those who by attachment to their country's interests unhesitatingly sacrifice what he calls the *crown of ataraxia*.

Looking out to sea, I was musing on my shames, old and new. The absurdity of self-concern when before your eyes stretches the greatest of all spectacles did not escape me. So I quickly changed the subject.

In the middle of the night, deep in the most trivial of books, I suddenly think of a long-dead friend whose judgment meant a great deal to me. What would he say if he saw how I spend my midnight hours? Only the viewpoint of the dead should matter, for only it is true—if we can even speak of truth in any circumstance whatever.

~

When you are born with a bad conscience, as if you had perpetrated exceptional misdeeds in another life, try as you will to commit only ordinary crimes in the course of this one, you still suffer guilt for which you can discover neither origin nor necessity.

~

Having done something particularly nasty, you are almost always dismayed. An impure dismay: as soon as you experience it, you start swaggering, proud of having felt such a noble indignation, even against yourself.

~

What you write gives only an incomplete image of what you are, because the words loom up and come to life only when you are at the highest or the lowest point of yourself.

~

Drawn and Quartered

Brooding just now on the *infinity of time*, I have not had the decency, paltry individual that I am, to eliminate myself. One should not be able to remain erect after perceiving all the terror such a cliché conceals.

~

Looking at someone's photographs taken at different ages, you glimpse why Time has been called a magician. The operations it accomplishes are incredible, stupefying—miracles, but miracles in reverse. This magician is actually a demolisher, a sadistic angel with the human face in his keeping.

~

While X is telephoning me from an asylum, I remind myself that you can do nothing for a brain, that it is impossible to set it in order again, that no one knows how to deal with billions of deteriorated or rebellious cells—in short, that one does not *repair* Chaos.

~

A concentrated or convulsive expression, dumb show of the ambitious, turns my stomach: in my youth I myself was a prey to frenzied ambitions, and now I am horrified to recognize in others the stig-mata of my first steps.

⁓

How to disentangle profundity from puffery in any obscure formulation? Clear thought stops short, a victim of its own probity; the other kind, vague and indecisive, extends into the distance and escapes by its suspect yet unassailable mystery.

⁓

In the hours without sleep, each moment is so full and so vacant that it suggests itself as a rival of Time.

⁓

The only *profound* thinkers are the ones who do not suffer from a sense of the ridiculous.

⁓

In the evils of life, the faculty of suicide is, ac-cording to Pliny, "the greatest benefit man has re-ceived." And he pities the gods for being unaware of such a temptation and such a piece of fortune.

To pity the supreme Being because He has not

the recourse of self-slaughter! An incomparable, a prodigious idea, which in and of itself consecrates the pagans' superiority over the madmen who were to supplant them.

To invoke wisdom is never to invoke *Christian* wisdom, for such a thing has never existed and never will exist. Two thousand futile years. A whole religion doomed before being born.

In my childhood, a profound shock when I heard my father, back from the cemetery, tell how a young mother who had lost her baby daughter burst out laughing at the moment the coffin was lowered into the grave. Fit of madness? Yes and no. For when we attend a funeral and the absolute deception is suddenly unmasked, do we not have a craving to react precisely like that mother? It is too much—it is almost a provocation: nature *exaggerates*. We conceive that we might collapse in hilarity.

The states whose cause is identifiable are not fruitful; only those states enrich us that occur without our knowing why. This is particularly true of extreme states, despondencies and joys that threaten our mind's integrity.

Stabs at Bewilderment

To publish groans, exclamations, fragments . . . makes everyone comfortable. The author thereby puts himself in a position of inferiority in relation to the reader, and the reader is grateful to him for it.

Each of us is entitled to claim the forebears who suit him, who *explain him* in his own eyes. How often have I not changed ancestors!

Indolence saves us from prolixity and thereby from the shamelessness inherent in production.

This old philosopher, when he wanted to dispose of someone, taxed him with being a "pessimist." As if he were saying "bastard." For him, a pessimist was anyone averse to utopia. That was how he branded every enemy of claptrap.

To contribute, in whatever form, to the ruin of whatever system, is the pursuit of a man who thinks only according to occasions and who will never consent to think for thinking's sake.

～

Time corrodes not only everything that lives, but even itself, as if, weary of continuing and exasperated by the Possible, its best part, it aspired to extirpate that as well.

～

There is no other world. Nor even this one. What, then, is there? The inner smile provoked in us by the patent nonexistence of both.

～

We cannot be sufficiently dubious of euphoria. The longer it lasts, the more we should be alarmed. Rarely justified, it flowers triumphantly, and not only without any serious reason but even without the slightest excuse. Instead of being delighted by its advent, we would do better to see it as a presage, a warning . . .

～

We are disturbed as long as we find ourselves confronted by a choice; as soon as we eliminate the very possibility of choosing and identify option with error, we tend toward the beatitude of a nonaffiliated being. When every conflict seems to be without basis, unreasonable, for whom and for what need we do battle, suffer, devour ourselves? But man is a strayed animal, and when he falls victim to doubt, if he should happen to take no further pleasure in attacking others, he turns on himself in order to inflict merciless tortures. Like Pascal, he converts doubt into an abyss and, introducing a somber note into Pyrrhonism, transforms the suspension of judgment into desperate interrogation.

Friendship is a pact, a convention. Two beings tacitly promise never to broadcast what each *really* thinks of the other. A kind of alliance based on compromises. When one of them publicly calls attention to the other's defects, the pact is declared null and void, the alliance broken. No friendship lasts if one of the partners ceases to play the game. In other words, no friendship tolerates an exaggerated proportion of honesty.

I was just over twenty, the philosopher I was talking to just over sixty. I don't know how we happened to tackle a theme as ungrateful as that of disease. "The last time I was ill," he acknowledged, "I must have been eleven. Since then, nothing at all . . ."

Fifty years of health! I had not nursed anything like a limitless admiration for my philosopher, but this avowal made me despise him instantaneously.

⚓

We are all of us in error, the humorists excepted. They alone have discerned, as though in jest, the inanity of all that is serious and even of all that is frivolous.

⚓

I shall be reconciled with myself only when I accept death the way one accepts an invitation to a dinner: with amused distaste.

⚓

Never importune someone except to announce a cataclysm or to make him a staggering compliment.

⚓

You must be cracked to lament man's extinction instead of chanting "Good Riddance!"

136

✎

A futile exception, a model no one abides by—such is the rank one should aspire to if one seeks to raise oneself in one's own eyes.

✎

If the skeptic admits that truth exists, he allows the innocent the illusion of believing they will some day possess it. As for me, he declares, I abide by appearances, I note what they are and adhere to them only to the degree that, as a living being, I cannot do otherwise. I act like other people, I perform the same deeds they do, but I identify myself with neither my words nor my actions, I bow to customs and laws, I pretend to share the convictions, *i.e.*, the prejudices, of my fellow citizens, while knowing that in the last analysis I am quite as *unreal* as they.

What then is the skeptic? —A ghost: a conformist ghost.

✎

We must live, you used to say, as if we were never going to die. —Didn't you know that's how everyone lives, including those obsessed with Death?

✎

137

To be present at one's diminution, to contemplate the *reasonable* edition of the hallucinated creature one has been!

∼

One generally concedes without too much embarrassment that one has reached the end of one's rope, but what one *never* admits is that one finds a certain pleasure in surviving oneself. And this clandestine, repugnant satisfaction is experienced by a good quarter of humanity . . .

∼

To deny original sin would be a proof that one has never reared children.

. . . I have not reared any, it is true, but I need merely recall my reactions as a child in order to dispel the slightest doubt as to the first of our stigmas.

∼

Incomprehensible blindness: this man, so vulnerable, flayed alive, is astonished that his progeniture should manifest disturbing signs. The delicate should never procreate, or if they do, should know at least toward what regrets they are heading.

∼

Stabs at Bewilderment

Life is more and less than boredom, though it is in boredom and by boredom that we discern what life is worth. Once boredom insinuates itself into you, once you fall under its invisible hegemony, everything else seems insignificant. The same might be said of suffering. Yes, indeed. But suffering is localized, whereas boredom evokes an evil without site or support, only that indefinable *nothing* that erodes you . . . A pure erosion, whose imperceptible effect slowly transforms you into a ruin unnoticed by others and almost unnoticed by yourself.

✎

Macabre obsessions afford no impediment to sexuality. On the contrary. We might look at the world the way a Buddhist monk does and still give evidence of a certain vigor . . . This strange compatibility makes illusory the claim to self-fulfillment by ascesis.

✎

It is our ailments which, fortunately, preserve us from abstract, conventional, "literary" bewilderments. In exchange, they gratify our bewilderments in the strict sense of the term.

✎

Drawn and Quartered

To have emitted more blasphemies than all the devils together, and to see yourself mistreated by certain organs, by the whims of a body, of a by-product!

꜍

He who has not suffered is not a *being*: at most, a creature.

꜍

We arrive at a very lofty idea of ourselves during the intervals when we scorn Death; on the other hand, when we consider Death with the pusillanimity of dread, we are truer, more *profound*, as happens each time we reject philosophy, attitude, lies.

꜍

Since my friend, whom I happened to meet while taking a walk, was determined to convince me that the "Divine" was present in all creatures without exception, I countered her with: "In that one too?", pointing at an intolerably vulgar-looking passerby. She could not answer, so true is it that theology and metaphysics abdicate before the authority of the paltriest detail.

꜍

All seeds, good and bad, are in us, save that of renunciation. Is it at all surprising that we should cling to things spontaneously and that it requires all the heroism we can muster for the converse impulse? If the faculty of renunciation had been granted to us, we should have no other effort to make than to *condescend* to exist.

To take sides or to resist doing so, to espouse a doctrine or to reject them all—the same pride in either case; with this difference, that we run a much greater risk of having to blush for ourselves in the former case than in the latter, *conviction* being at the source of virtually all deviations, as of all humiliations.

"Your book is a failure."—"No doubt, but you are forgetting that I wanted it to be one, and that it could hardly be a *success* otherwise."

To die at sixty or at eighty is harder than at ten or at thirty. Habituation to life, there's the rub. For life is a vice—the greatest one of all. Which explains why we have so much difficulty ridding ourselves of it.

141

Drawn and Quartered

❧

When I happen to be satisfied with everything, even with God and myself, I immediately react like the man who, on a brilliant day, torments himself because the sun is bound to explode in a few billion years.

❧

"What is truth?" is a fundamental question. But what is it compared to "How to endure life?" And even this one pales beside the next: "How to endure oneself?" —That is the crucial question to which no one is in a position to give us an answer.

❧

What inadvertence, to begin describing, at the bedside of a dangerously ill friend, a stroll I once took through Passy cemetery and my conversation with the gravedigger on duty! I stopped short in the middle of a joke, which merely emphasized the untimeliness of my chatter. We can approach such subjects only at the dinner table, when we are in a festive mood and need a few funereal allusions to give ourselves a better appetite.

❧

Stabs at Bewilderment

The only moments that deserve to survive the collapse of our memory are those when we cannot forgive ourselves for not being the First or the Last.

Those who have reproached this philosopher for signing contradictory protests, for subscribing simultaneously or successively to certain conflicting parties or theses, without considering his own options, have forgotten that this is just what philosophy should be. For what is the use of devoting oneself to it if one does not enter into the reasons of other men? Of two enemies at odds, it is unlikely that only one should be in the right. When we listen to them one after the other, we yield, if we are in good faith, to the arguments of each, at the risk of looking like a weathercock, of being, in short, *too much* of a philosopher.

What to think of other people? I ask myself this question each time I make a new acquaintance. So strange does it seem to me that we exist, and that we consent to exist.

At the Jardin des Plantes, I stood for a long time meeting the immemorial gaze of an alligator's eyes.

What enchants me in these reptiles is their impenetrable hebetude, which allies them to stones: as if they came *before* life, preceded without heralding it, as if they even fled from it . . .

≈

"What is evil? It is what is done with a view to happiness in this world."
Abhidarmakoshavyâkhyâ
It took a title like that to warrant such an answer.

≈

In hell, the least populous but the severest circle of all must be the one where you cannot forget Time for a single moment.

≈

"It is of no importance to know who I am since some day I shall no longer be"—that is what each of us should answer those who bother about our identity and desire at any price to coop us up in a category or a definition.

≈

Everything is nothing, including the consciousness of nothing.

144

That mysterious, profound, complicated, ineffable race that has excelled and excels in everything, even in failure, will have an end worthy of itself and will know calamities it need not blush for.

Homer has been taken to task (Heraclitus himself claimed he deserved a whipping) because he made no bones about it: his gods, as much as his mortals, behaved like scoundrels. Philosophy had not yet appeared to weaken them, to sweeten them, to make them *suitable*. Young, strong, lively, they communicated with human beings in the passion of the tragic. The dawn of a mythology, as history testifies, is what is most to be feared. The ideal would be *exhausted* gods, and eternal. Unfortunately, having reached the stage where weariness succeeds ferocity, gods do not subsist for long. Others—vigorous, ruthless—will replace them. And so we subside from the serene into the sinister, from repose into epic.

Abominable Clio![22]

Anything but discouraging, the notion that no one will remember the accident we have been, that not the slightest trace will remain of a *self*, that collector of torments no torturer has ever dared dream of.

❧

Incapable of living in the moment, only in the future and the past, in anxiety and regret! Now, theologians are categorical on the subject: this is the condition and the very definition of the sinner. A man without a present tense.

❧

Everything that happens is at once natural and inconceivable.

This conclusion is unavoidable, whether we consider great or trivial events.

❧

To waken every morning in the frame of mind of a Roman of the Republic the day after the battle of Pharsalus.

❧

Stabs at Bewilderment

One disgust, then another—to the point of losing the use of speech and even of the mind.

The greatest exploit of my life is to be still alive.

If the waves began to reflect, they would suppose that they were advancing, that they had a goal, that they were making progress, that they were working for the Sea's good, and they would not fail to elaborate a philosophy as stupid as their zeal.

If we had an infallible perception of what we are, we might have just enough courage to go to bed, but certainly not enough to get up.

I have always struggled, with the sole intention of ceasing to struggle. Result: zero.

Lucky those who are unaware that to mature is to witness the aggravation of our incoherences, and that this is the only progress we should be allowed to boast of.

147

Drawn and Quartered

Everything I have ventured, everything I have held forth on all my life is indissociable from what I have experienced. I have invented nothing, I have merely been the secretary of my sensations.

IV ~

Epictetus: "Pleasure consists not in acquiring and enjoying but in not desiring." —If wisdom is defined as opposition to Desire, it is because wisdom is concerned to make us superior to the ordinary disappointments as well as to the dramatic ones, inseparable, on either count, from the phenomenon of desiring, expecting, hoping. It is chiefly from the capital disappointments that wisdom seeks to preserve us, having specialized in the art of confronting or enduring the "blows of fate." Of all the Ancients, it was the Stoics who carried this art furthest. According to them, the wise man possesses an exceptional status in the universe: the gods are secured from evils; the wise man is *above*, he is invested with a force that allows him to conquer all his desires. The gods are still subjected to theirs, they live in servitude; he alone escapes them. How does he raise himself to the unwonted, how does he manage to outclass all beings, mortal and divine? Apparently he does not immediately discern the bearing of his status: he is certainly above men and gods, but he must wait a certain while before realizing the fact. We have no difficulty admitting that it is not easy for him to understand his position, especially since we wonder when and where we have seen so prodigious an anomaly, such a specimen of virtue and pride. The wise man, Seneca claims, exceeds Jupiter in being able to scorn the privileges of this world and in refusing to benefit by them, while Jupiter, having no need of them and dismissing them from the start, has neither the occasion nor the merit of triumphing over them.

Never has man been set so high. Where are we to seek the origins of so exaggerated a vision? —Born in Cyprus, Zeno, the father of Stoicism, was a Hellenized Phoenician who kept his half-breed status to the end of his days. Antisthenes, founder of the Cynic school (of which Stoicism is the improved or denatured version, as you like), was born in Athens, his mother a Thracian woman. In these doctrines there is clearly something non-Greek, a style of life and thought deriving from other horizons. One is tempted to assert that everything which astonishes and jars in an advanced civilization is the product of newcomers, immigrants, marginal types eager to dazzle. . . .

With the advent of Christianity the sage ceases to set an example; in his place, we begin to venerate the saint, a convulsive variety of the sage and one thereby more accessible to the masses. Despite its diffusion and its prestige, Stoicism remained the apanage of refined milieus, the ethic of patricians. Once they had vanished, it too would disappear. The cult of wisdom would be eclipsed for a long interval, one might almost say forever. We shall not recognize it, at any rate, in the modern systems conceived, each one, not so much by an *anti-sage* as by a *non-sage*.

If, instead of dying at thirty-two, Julian the Apostate had reached a great age, would he have succeeded in smothering the dawning superstition? We may doubt it, as he himself must have done, for if he had believed it possible, he would not have stupidly risked his life against the Parthians when a much more important combat lay ahead of him. Certainly he felt that his enterprise was doomed to failure . . . Why not die somewhere on the Empire's periphery?

How to disentangle those things that depend on us from those that do not? I have no notion.

Sometimes I feel responsible for everything I do, though when I think of it I have merely followed an impulse of which I was anything but the master; at other times, I believe myself to be conditioned and subservient, yet I have merely conformed to a reasoning conceived outside of any and all constraint, even a . . . rational constraint.

Impossible to know how and when one is free, how and when one is manipulated. If, each time, one wanted to examine oneself in order to identify the precise nature of an action, one would end up with vertigo rather than with a conclusion. From which it will be deduced that if there were a solution to the problem of free will, philosophy would have no reason to exist.

We can conceive of eternity only by eliminating all the perishable, all that *counts* for us. Eternity is absence, being that fills none of the functions of being; it is privation erected into . . . something or other, hence it is nothing or, at most, an estimable fiction.

No more than authentic ecstasy, euphoria, a frivolous ecstasy, is not a natural phenomenon but a deviation, a heresy, an aberrant and yet unhoped-for state, for which we must pay; which is why, each time we experience it we must expect an *"expiation,"* either immediate or belated, in any case inevitable. *Jubilation,* in whatever form, involves, to various degrees, migraine, nausea, or something as pitiable, as degrading.

Stabs at Bewilderment

Undeniable sign of spiritual nonfulfillment: every passionate reaction to blame, that twinge at the heart whenever we are reproached in one way or another. This is the cry of the old Adam in each of us, it proves we have not yet conquered our origins. So long as we do not aspire to be scorned, we are like *the others*, like those precisely whom we scorn.

X, who instead of looking at things directly has spent his life juggling with concepts and abusing abstract terms, now that he must envisage his own death, is in desperate straits. Fortunately for him, he flings himself, as is his custom, into abstractions, into commonplaces illustrated by jargon. A glamorous hocus-pocus, such is philosophy. But ultimately, *everything is hocus-pocus*, except for this very assertion that participates in an order of propositions one dares not question because they emanate from an unverifiable certitude, one somehow *anterior* to the brain's career.

It was winter, just after the Luxembourg gardens had opened for the day. No one, except for one couple: a scrawny, energetic old man and a girl who looked like a milkmaid. The fog was so thick that even at close range they seemed to be ghosts. Every ten steps they would stop to embrace, rushing into each other's arms with an ardor I had never seen equalled. Was it joy or despair, this frenzy so early in the morning, an hour so unpropitious to such effusions? And if they let themselves go like this out of doors, how to imagine them in the intimacy of four walls? Following them, I kept telling myself that all acrobatics *à deux* was error, delusion, but a delusion of sorts, an unclassifiable mistake.

～

To torment oneself in the middle of the night, to perform every known sort of exercise, to swallow pills, tablets, capsules—why? In hopes of eclipsing that phenomenon, that deadly apparition known as consciousness. Only a conscious being, only a weakling, could have invented such an expression as to be *engulfed* in sleep, a gulf indeed but a rare, inaccessible one, a forbidden, sealed gulf, into which we would so like to vanish!

～

Young, I dreamed of overturning everything. I have reached an age where one no longer overturns—where one *is* overturned. Between the two extremes, what has happened? Something which is nothing and yet everything: that unformulable evidence that one is no longer the same, that one will never again be the same.

~

Each individual who dies takes the universe with him: thereby everything is suppressed, everything: a supreme justice which legitimizes and rehabilitates death. So let us depart without regret, since nothing survives us, our consciousness being the sole and unique reality: with it abolished, everything is abolished, even if we *know* that this is not objectively true and that in fact nothing consents to follow us, nothing deigns to perish with us.

~

In a park, this sign: "Because of the condition *(age and disease)* of the trees, they are being replaced."

The war of generations, even here! The simple fact of living, even in the vegetable kingdom, is assigned a fatal coefficient. Hence we are content to breathe only when we forget we are alive.

~

Nothing is so stimulating as the narrative of a conversion. Instead of tonics, we should prescribe the confessions of the illuminated, the *regenerate*: what vitality, what appetite for illusion, what brilliance in every new—even in every old—lie! At the contact with truth, on the other hand, everything darkens and turns against you, as if its rôle were to make you lose all your resources.

It is said that in China, the sensitive take (or rather took, for this all reeks of the past) a particular and delicate pleasure in listening closely to the ticking of a clock. Such an apparently *material* attention to Time is in reality a highly philosophical exercise, from which one obtains, upon giving oneself up to it, marvelous results in the immediate—in the immediate *only*.

Boredom, the corrosive product of the obsession with Time, would triumph over granite itself, and you ask weaklings like me to deal with it!

A whole period of my life seems scarcely imaginable to me today, so alien to me has it become. How could I have been the man I was? My old enthusiasms seem ridiculous to me—all that fever expended in vain.

If I extended this way of looking at things to the whole of my life, would I not come to the point of regarding everything I have experienced as a hoax or as error? And if, for instance, we had this perception at the moment of death? But it is not necessary to wait for that moment: thanks to certain awakenings, we realize that the foundations of an existence are as fragile as the appearances which mask them, and that we do not even have the resource of considering them rotten, since they are quite simply nonexistent.

After all, why *should* ordinary people want to contemplate the End, especially when we see the condition of those who do?

We forget the body, but the body does not forget us. Cursed memory of the organs!

I have always deplored both my acquiescences and my phobias! If only I had flung myself into the orgy of abstention!

What can be said, lacks reality. Only what fails to make its way into words exists and counts.

Woe to the book you can read without constantly wondering about the author!

Nietzsche, proud of his "instinct," of his "nose," may have realized the importance of a Dostoievski, but how many mistakes he made, how many writers of the second and third rank he adored! What is dumbfounding is that he too supposed that behind Shakespeare lurked Bacon, the least *poet* of the philosophers!

If we compiled a list of all his howlers, we would soon realize that they equal Voltaire's in number and gravity, though with this extenuating circumstance, for Nietzsche: he was often mistaken because he *wanted* to be or seem frivolous, whereas Voltaire had no need to make the effort.

To think is to run after insecurity, to be *demoralized* for grandiose trifles, to immure oneself in abstractions with a martyr's avidity, to hunt up complications the way others pursue collapse or gain. The thinker is by definition *keen for torment.*

≠

If death were not a kind of solution, the living would certainly have found some means of avoiding it.

≠

For Alcmaeon of Crotona, a contemporary of Pythagoras, disease was due to a breakdown of equilibrium between hot and cold, wet and dry, the contrary elements which constitute us. When one of them prevails and dictates, disease results; hence it is only the "monarchy," as he said, of one of these elements, whereas health would result from an equality among them.

This vision has something true about it: no disequilibrium that does not appear from an abusive preeminence of one organ or another at the expense of the rest, from its *ambition* to impose itself, to proclaim, to *shout* its presence: by dint of contention, of insistence, it deranges the whole organism and compromises its future. A sick organ is an organ that emancipates itself from the body and tyrannizes over it, destroys the body and itself, and this solely in order *to show off,* to turn itself into a star.

It makes no sense to say that death is the goal of life. But what else is there to say?

I try to imagine the moment when I shall have conquered the *last* desire.

Too bad that God has not kept a monopoly of "me" and that He should have entitled us to speak in our own name. It would have been so simple to spare us the scourge of "I"!

"To follow one's inclination rather than to make one's way." This phrase of Talleyrand's haunts me. For years, opposing my "inclination," I turned to expressions of wisdom alien to my nature, concerned to neutralize my bad tendencies instead of letting myself go, dedicating myself to . . . myself. It is a seducer, it is the genius of *salvation* which has tempted me, and in yielding to it, even if only momentarily, I have contributed as best I could to the debilitation of the man I was and whom I should have remained.

We are ourselves only by mobilizing all our defects, siding with our weaknesses, following our "inclination." As soon as we seek our "way" and elect some noble model, we botch ourselves, we miss the point . . .

The originality of a being is identified with his particular way of losing his footing. Primacy of noninterference: let each live and die as he wants, as if he had the luck to resemble no one, as if he were a blessed monster. Leave the others the way they are, and they will be grateful to you. If you seek their happiness at all costs, they will be revenged.

One is *true* only to the degree that one is encumbered by no talent.

We regret not having had the courage to make such and such a decision; we regret much more having made one—any one. Better no action than the consequences of an action!

According to Isaac the Syrian: "As for those who have attained perfection, this is their sign: if they were to be given to the flames ten times a day for love of the human race, they would find that this is not often enough."

Those hermits so prompt to sacrifice themselves, so ready to pray for everything and everyone, for the reptiles themselves—what generosity and what perversity! And what leisure! One must have time to burn and the curiosity of a lunatic to waste pity on everything that stirs. Ascesis—a sublime depravity . . .

Any invalid thinks more than a thinker. Sickness is disjunction, hence reflexion. It always severs us from something, and sometimes from everything. Even an idiot who experiences a violent sensation of pain thereby exceeds his idiocy; he is conscious of his sensation and sets himself above it, and perhaps above himself, from the moment he feels that it is *he* who is suffering. Similarly, there must be, among the beasts, various degrees of consciousness, according to the intensity of the disease from which they suffer.

Nothing is more mysterious than the destiny of a body.

⤙

Time has an absolute meaning only for the incurable.

⤙

To define nothing is among the skeptic's obligations. But what can we oppose to the swagger that follows the merest definition we happen to have found? To define is one of the most inveterate of our madnesses, and it must have been born with the first word.

⤙

All things considered, philosophy is not so contemptible: to hide oneself under more or less objective truths, to disclose oppressions that apparently do not concern us, to cultivate faceless dreads, to camouflage calls for help by the splendors of language . . . Philosophy? An anonymous cry . . .

⤙

Conversation is fruitful only between minds given to consolidating their perplexities.

⤙

"You really should come to the house—one of these days we might die without having seen each other again." —"Since we have to die in any case, what's the use of seeing each other again?"

～

We fall asleep with a contentment which is indescribable, we slide into oblivion and are happy to lose ourselves there. If we waken reluctantly, it is because we do not leave unconsciousness, the one true paradise, without pain. Which is to say that man is fulfilled only when he ceases to be man.

～

"Slander," proclaims the Talmud, "is a sin as grave as idolatry, incest and murder." —Very well. But if it is possible to live without killing, without sleeping with one's mother and without sacrificing to the golden calf, by what subterfuge can one get through a single day without hating one's neighbor and hating oneself in him?

～

When one gets up in a bad mood, it is inevitable that one should make certain dreadful discoveries, if only by observing oneself.

Stabs at Bewilderment

A huge exhibition of insects. Just at the point of going in, I turned around and left. I wasn't in the mood to *admire*.

A terrible yet endurable mortification: to be born among a people that will never be *mentioned*.

Everyone is mistaken, everyone lives in illusion. At best, we can admit a scale of fictions, a hierarchy of unrealities, giving preference to one rather than to another; but to *choose*, no, definitely not that . . .

Only the perception of the Void allows us to triumph over death. For if everything lacks reality, why should death be allowed it?

Even more than in the poem, it is in the aphorism that the word is god.

Drawn and Quartered

*

Who cares tomorrow about an idea we had entertained the day before? —After any night, we are no longer the same, and we cheat when we play out the farce of continuity. —The *fragment*, no doubt a disappointing genre, but the only honest one.

*

Each of us expects to be finished off by injuries or by the years, whereas it would be so simple to put an end *to all that*. Individuals, like empires, favor a long, shameful end.

*

How explain that everything we want to do and, still more, everything we *do*, seems to us crucial? The folly which made God emerge from His aboriginal sloth is to be recognized in the least of our gestures—and that is our great excuse.

*

All morning, I did nothing but repeat: "Man is an abyss, man is an abyss." —I could not, alas, find anything better.

*

Stabs at Bewilderment

Old age, after all, is merely the punishment for having lived.

~

Boredom, which seems to search out everything to its root, actually searches out nothing, because it descends only into itself and sounds only its own void.

~

Hope is the *normal* form of delirium.

~

My deficiency in *being*. One cannot last without foundations, though I do my damnedest.

~

Try as I will, I don't see *what* might exist . . .

~

The hardest thing is not to attack one of those great insoluble questions, but instead to send someone a delicate little note saying at once nothing and everything . . .

167

A curious dream over which I prefer not to linger. Someone or other would have dissected it. What a mistake! Let the nights bury the nights.

When we love a language as much for its manifest virtues as for its latent ones, the sacrilegious way linguists treat it makes them so odious that we should gladly side with the first regime that would hang them as a matter of course.

One can quote Pascal only in French. He is the only prose writer who, even when perfectly translated, loses his *accent*, his substance, his uniqueness, and this because the *Pensées*, from being recited so often, have turned into refrains, into clichés. Unheard-of refrains, dazzling clichés. Yet we cannot manipulate clichés, whether brilliant or worthless, we must serve them up untouched, in their original and trite expression, like hackneyed lightning bolts.

It has been claimed that "self-acceptance" is indispensable if one wants to produce, "to create."

The contrary is true. It is because one does not accept oneself that one begins to work, that one considers others and, above all, oneself, in order to know who is this stranger encountered at every step, who refuses to reveal his identity and whom one can be rid of only by coming to grips with his secrets, by violating and profaning them.

A light and rarefied, *unbreathable* book, one that would be on the brink of everything, and be addressed to no one . . .

To collect one's thoughts, to polish up certain denuded truths—anyone can manage that, more or less; but the *edge*, without which a pithy shortcut is only a statement, a mere maxim, requires a touch of virtuosity, even of charlatanism. *Ingenious minds* should not risk themselves here.

An author who claims to write for posterity must be a bad one. We should never know *for whom* we write.

To reflect is to acknowledge a certain impossibility. To meditate is to give this acknowledgment a patent of nobility.

Which is better: to be fulfilled in the literary order, or in the spiritual—to have talent, or possess an inner power?

The second formula seems preferable, being rarer and more enriching. Talent is doomed to exhaustion; on the other hand, inner power increases with the years, it can even reach its apogee at the very moment one expires.

According to Julius Capitolinus, his biographer, Marcus Aurelius raised his wife's lovers "to the greatest honors."

Wisdom borders on extravagance; moreover a sage deserves the name only insofar as he is an original, a real character.

If equilibrium, in all its forms, smothers the mind, health extinguishes it altogether.

170

I have never been able to find out what *being* means, except sometimes in eminently nonphilosophical moments.

⚬

We are fulfilled only when we aspire to nothing, when we are impregnated by that nothing to the point of intoxication.

⚬

If I were to go blind, what would bother me the most would be no longer to be able to stare idiotically at the passing clouds.

⚬

It is not *normal* to be alive, since the living being as such exists and is real only when *threatened*. Death in short is no more than the cessation of an anomaly.

⚬

The child who does not smile at two and a half should inspire certain anxieties. The smile is therefore a sign of health, of balance. The madman, it is true, laughs more than he smiles.

⚬

Drawn and Quartered

We live in the false as long as we have not suffered. But when we begin to suffer, we enter the truth only to regret the false.

~

Looking at this accumulation of graves, it seems that people have no other concern than to die.

~

A stranger wants to know if I still see X. —I answer that I do not, and I list the reasons for my estrangement with such precision that, waking up, I marvel that a dream can expound a situation so rigorously whereas everything else plunges into the chaos, the grotesquerie, and the anarchy of sleep. It is the *logic of rancor*, of something that defies everything, even Chaos.

~

Can one be *tempered* without falling into fanaticism? Unfortunately *spiritual power* inevitably turns in this direction. The "hero" himself is only a disguised fanatic.

~

Stabs at Bewilderment

All morning—odd sensations: desire to show myself, to make projects, to assert, *to work*. Delirium, trance, intoxication, unconquerable euphoria. Fortunately, fatigue comes to sober me up, to call me to order, to the nothingness of each moment.

*

The worst is not ennui nor despair but their encounter, their collision. To be crushed between the two!

*

Am I a skeptic? Am I a flagellant?—I shall never know, and so much the better.

*

He who has not had the good luck to die young will leave only a caricature of his pride behind.

*

Desolation is so linked to what I feel that it acquires the facility of a reflex.

*

173

"To make an attempt upon one's days"—how accurate this French expression for suicide. What we possess is just that: days, days, and that is all we can attack.

～

In the usual boredom, we desire nothing, we lack even the curiosity to weep; in the excess of boredom it is just the contrary, for this excess incites us to action, and weeping is an action.

～

In this Norman port, they have just caught a huge fish they call "Moonfish," which must have been carried here by some warm current, for it is not native to these regions. Lying on the dock, it shivers and writhes, then gives up and stops moving. An agony without pangs, a *model agony*.

～

If there were not this abject stupor in confronting death, only a few madmen would resist the *charm* it cannot fail to exert upon any normally constituted individual.

～

174

Theology distinguishes essential glory from accidental glory. We know and understand only the second. Only the first matters.

Every *project* is a camouflaged form of slavery.

To resign oneself or to blow out one's brains, that is the choice one faces at certain moments. In any case, the only real dignity is that of exclusion.

I began to decline the moment ecstasy no longer visited me, when the extraordinary left my life. Instead came a sterile and anxious astonishment which will ultimately be devalued, degraded to the point of losing everything, even anxiety.

It is not true that the idea of death rids us of all vile thoughts. It does not even make us blush for having such thoughts.

Nothing corrects us for anything. The ambitious man remains such until his dying breath, and would pursue fame and fortune even if the globe were about to explode.

⚬

At this moment, I am *alone*. What more can I want? A more intense happiness does not exist. Yes: that of hearing, by dint of silence, my solitude *enlarge*.

⚬

According to Sumerian mythology, the flood was the punishment the gods inflicted on man because of the noise he made. —What would I not give to know how they will reward him for today's racket?

⚬

I have spent so long circling round the idea of death that I should be lying if I *located myself* in relation to it. What is certain is that I cannot do without it, cannot brood over anything else . . .

⚬

Timidity, inexhaustible source of misfortunes in practical life, is the direct, even the unique cause of all inner wealth.

⚬

Man, a former animal but an animal still, is better and worse than the animal. The superman, if he were possible, would be better and worse than man. An *undesirable* of the most disturbing sort. To count on his coming is sheer frivolity.

What folly to link oneself with beings and things, and what greater folly to suppose that one can loose oneself from them. To have sought renunciation at any price and still to be only a *candidate* for renunciation.

Only the verbal apanage of metaphysics—if one still condescends to make use of it—manages to relieve existence somewhat.

As soon as we consider it without any sort of pomp or paraph, existence comes down to a wretched wonder.

Death is the solidest thing life has invented, so far.

Drawn and Quartered

The crucial moment of the historical drama is out of our reach. We are merely its harbingers, its heralds—the *trumpets* of a Judgment without a Judge.

~

Time, accomplice of exterminators, disposes of morality. Who, today, bears a grudge against Nebuchadnezzar?

~

For a nation to count, its average must be high. What we call *civilization* or simply *society* is nothing but the excellent quality of the mediocre individuals who compose it.

~

Torquemada[23] was *sincere*, hence inflexible, inhuman. The corrupt popes were charitable, like all who can be bought.

~

Their ancient laws forbade the Jews to predict the future. A just prohibition. For if they had foreseen what was before them, would they have had the strength to sustain themselves, to be themselves, to confront the shocks of such a destiny?

~

"The powers do not act below, but from above, working downward," says one hermetic author. This may be true, but in no way applies to the historical process, where *submergence* is the law.

~

No system, no doctrine of action can appeal to Epicurus, adversary of any upheaval, any promise, any ostentation linked to the merest step forward. No one has ever cited him on the barricades. His position is one of withdrawal, and if he wanted to reform men, it was to lead them to *less* than what they pursue. The most intractable enemy of zeal, puncturer *par excellence* of the Best and of the Worst.

~

A Chinese proverb: "When one dog begins barking at a shadow, ten thousand make it into a reality." —An epigraph to any commentary on ideologies.

~

It is a conspicuous advantage to be able to contemplate the end of a religion. What, compared to this, is the fall of a nation and even of a civilization? To be present at the eclipse of a god and of the age-old enormities attached to him also provokes a jubilation that few generations, in the course of history, have had the luck to know or even guess.

We are predetermined but we are not automatons. We are more or less free, within an imperfect fatality. Our conflicts with others and with ourselves open a breach in our prison, and it is very true that there exist degrees of freedom, as there exist degrees of rottenness.

To grant life more importance than it has is the mistake committed in sagging systems; as a consequence, no one is ready to sacrifice himself to defend them, and they collapse under the first blows perpetrated upon them. This is even more true of nations in general. Once they begin to hold life *sacred*, it abandons them, it ceases to be on their side.

Freedom is an expense, freedom exhausts, while oppression causes us to muster our forces, prevents the waste of energy resulting from the free man's faculty of externalizing, of projecting *the good* outside himself. We see why slaves always win in the long run. Masters, to their defeat, manifest themselves, drain themselves of their existence, *express themselves*: the unconstrained exercise of their gifts, of their advantages, reduces them to the state of phantoms. Freedom will have devoured them.

Serfs, this nation built the cathedrals; emancipated, it constructs one horror after another.

Man is *unacceptable*.

To flee the deluders, never to proffer any kind of *yes!*

Every utopia about to be realized resembles a cynical dream.

Only a *superficial* religion—or ideology—is tolerable. Unfortunately history affords very few.

181

Drawn and Quartered

⚕

In order to mold man, it was not with water but with tears that Prometheus mixed his clay . . . And we still speak, apropos of the Ancients, of serenity, a word which in no period has had any content whatever.

⚕

To be infatuated with lost causes leads one to suppose that they are all just that, and one is not entirely mistaken.

⚕

"The madman's life is joyless, bestirred, and betakes itself entirely toward what is to come." This remark of Seneca's, quoted by Montaigne, can serve to show that the obsession with history's meaning is a source of confusions, as indeed it is: to follow or to oppose the current comes down to the same thing, since in both cases we still peer into the future, as consenting victims or reluctant ones.

⚕

From earliest times, man has craved a definitive conflagration, hoping to get rid of history once and for all. What is remarkable is that he should have formed this dream so early, at his beginnings in fact, when events could not yet have overwhelmed him beyond measure. We must deduce that the terror of what lay in wait for him, of what the ages held in reserve, was so intense, and so distinct, that it quickly changed into certainty, into vision, into hope . . .

"I had the instinct of a fatal outcome." —This phrase, uttered at Saint Helena, is one that anyone is entitled to pronounce: it even suits the human race in general, whose obscure character it explains, along with its ambiguities, vague and tragic alike, as well as its panting advance, its progress toward the final stage, toward the kingdom of ghosts and puppets.

Novalis[24] says: "It depends on us to make the world accord with our will." This is precisely the contrary of everything we can think and feel at the end of a life, and, with all the more reason, at the end of history . . .

Notes and References

1. Charron: sixteenth-century French moralist.
2. Rancé: seventeenth-century French religious reformer.
3. Mommsen: nineteenth-century German historian.
4. Mme. du Deffand: (1697–1780) French marquise known for her literary salons.
5. Duclos: eighteenth-century French writer.
6. Mme. de Genlis: (1747–1830) French woman of letters.
7. Cardinal Dubois: (1656-1752) French statesman.
8. Duchesse de Choiseul: wife of Choiseul (1719–1785), Minister to Louis XV.
9. Chamfort: eighteenth-century French writer and aphorist.
10. Rivarol: eighteenth-century French writer and journalist.
11. Marquise de Prie: (1698–1727), mistress of the Duc de Bourbon, active in political circles.

12. Ahriman: the spirit of evil in Zoroastrianism.
13. *Origins of Christianity*: written by Ernest Renan (1823–1892).
14. Carl-Gustav Carus: nineteenth-century German philosopher.
15. Léon Bloy: nineteenth-century French writer and polemicist.
16. Meister Eckhart: (1260–1327) German philosopher and mystic.
17. Rig-Veda: the most ancient collection of Hindu sacred verses.
18. Dangeau: seventeenth-century French chronicler.
19. Epictetus: first-century Greek philosopher.
20. Origen: first-century Greek father of the Church.
21. Marquise de Brinvilliers: (1630–1676) French noblewoman known for the murders she committed and for Mme. de Sévigné's account of her execution.
22. Abominable Clio!: a response to Giraudoux's phrase: *adorable Clio*.
23. Torquemada: head of the Spanish Inquisition.
24. Novalis: eighteenth-century German Romantic poet.